195

A PLACE OF HER OWN
The Story of Elizabeth Garrett
by
Ruth K. Hall

Sunstone Press
Santa Fe, New Mexico

ACKNOWLEDGMENTS

My sincerest thanks to George Fitzpatrick, Albuquerque, New Mexico, for his help and encouragement. To Mrs. Frederick R. Brown, Albuquerque, for the loan of photographs. To Mrs. Norman Blower, El Paso, Texas, for pictures and information. To Mrs. Howard Murphy, Roswell, New Mexico, for invaluable information. Special thanks to my sister, Betty Johnson, who typed the manuscript.

Library of Congress Cataloging in Publication Data:

Hall, Ruth K.
    A place of her own.

    Bibliography: .
    1. Garrett, Elizabeth, 1885?-1947. 2. Composers—United States—Biography. 3. Musicians, Blind—United States—Biography. I. Title.
ML410.Gl693H3   1983   784.5'0092'4 [B]   83-5104
ISBN 0-913270-68-7

Published in 1983 by Sunstone Press / Post Office Box 2321 / Santa Fe, New Mexico 87504-2321

*To Richard my husband
whose encouragement made it possible.*

INTRODUCTION

Elizabeth Garrett was born blind. She never saw with her eyes. Everything she learned came to her through her senses of touch, hearing, smelling and that elusive sixth sense which some call "feeling." For those of us who came to know trees and flowers, sky and earth, friends, family, mountains, desert, dogs and horses merely by looking this is almost incomprehensible. But, until she learned Braille, and frequently thereafter, Elizabeth gained knowledge of the things about her by listening to other people describe them.

When someone says to a sighted person, "Look at those roses," they look and see. For Elizabeth a description was necessary. When she didn't "see" clearly what was meant, she asked questions. Her whole life was spent in conversation so that she might see everything.

The author has written the larger part of this biography in the form of dialogue. Lengthy descriptions of people and places, related by a narrator, would not give the reader a feel for Elizabeth's world. She lived with sound. Other people's voices were her eyes; she saw through them.

Wm. Farrington

FOREWORD

Elizabeth Garrett, blind singer and composer, was the daughter of Pat Garrett, famous frontier sheriff who has been immortalized in western pictures, song and story as the man who shot the notorious outlaw, Billy the Kid.

Elizabeth was born in a turbulent era of New Mexico's territorial days, the third of eight children. Her mother was a native woman of Spanish-Indian family.

Elizabeth never knew physical sight, but she was keenly aware of the world around her. She felt no self-pity, but rather a deep sense of gratitude for her health, her talents, her close knit family, and the heritage of her beloved state.

Music was in her blood. Many compositions, which included Spanish-Mexican, Indian, cowboy and state folklore songs, as well as songs of nature and inspiring religious themes were the children of her soul and brain. As an envoy of song, her glorious voice extolled the beauties and romance of New Mexico as long as she lived.

She received many honors in return for her contributions to the cultural growth of the Southwest. She once said: "My father tried to bring peace and harmony to our country with his guns; I would like to do my part with my music."

This account of her life is written from personal recollections of close friends and members of Miss Garrett's family, with careful research by the author into the facts and the historical and geographical background.

AUTHOR'S NOTE

This book is intended primarily for young readers, with the hope that a fuller interest in the history and geography of New Mexico might be engendered. It is hoped, too, that the story of a handicapped half-Chicano girl, born at the close of a turbulent era, who was determined to make a place for herself and to become independent and self-supporting, may be of inspirational value to young people.

Only close friends of the family knew the side of Pat Garrett's character that is portrayed here. Many stories have been told about this controversial man, ranging from fact to fiction, and often picturing him as ruthless, cruel, even dissolute. However, Elizabeth's own story, as related to friends and confidants, refutes much of this. We learn that he was devoted to his family and instilled in his children a love for learning and a strong feeling of loyalty to each other and to their state and country.

Except for the brief period in El Paso, he was never financially secure, and yet all the children except Poe, who was physically unable to attend school, received college educations in a time when this was a difficult accomplishment. This fact plainly reflects Pat Garrett's influence on his family.

A PLACE OF HER OWN
The Story of Elizabeth Garrett

Chapter 1

A PLACE OF HER OWN
The Story of Elizabeth Garrett

CHAPTER 1

She was born October 12 in the mid-1880s* on a ranch at Eagle Creek, a remote section of vast Lincoln County in the Territory of New Mexico.

She was a healthy baby, dimpled and chubby, with dark hair and eyes and cheeks as pink as a wild rose.

"What shall we name her?" Mr. and Mrs. Garrett asked each other. Five year old Ida had been given a good family name, and little Poe, almost two, was named for a close friend of Mr. Garrett.

"Let's call her Elizabeth," her father said. "It means Child of God." And his wife agreed; it seemed an appropriate name for this perfect little girl.

The baby was several weeks old when her mother made an alarming discovery. Her dark eyes didn't follow moving objects; there was no reaction to sudden bright light. Something was wrong!

The nearest doctors were miles away, but visits were arranged and anxious consultations held. At last, shocked and saddened, they were forced to accept the doctors' verdict. Little Elizabeth was blind!

Patrick Garrett was a man of strong will and determination. "She must grow up as a normal child," he said.

"But how can she?" Mrs. Garrett wept. "She cannot see! How can she be normal?"

"In this house, we will never use the word *blind*," he said firmly. "We must teach her to be like any child, happy and free from fear. When she is old enough, she must go to a special school. But that will come later."

Pat Garrett was well known throughout the Territory as the former Sheriff of Lincoln County, a fearless man of the law who had helped to rid the wild frontier of outlaws and cattle rustlers. Since his marriage to pretty Apolinaria Gutierrez, however, he had settled down to ranching.

Mrs. Garrett was sure there had never been a better husband than her tall, blue-eyed Pat. So clever, too; building their house himself, carefully selecting only the best logs. And the roof, sturdy and strong, with a foot-deep layer of mountain soil on top for insulation. There was never a prettier roof than theirs. In summer, a colorful profusion of wild flowers sprang from that soil, giving

*Believed to have been 1885

the cabin a look of riotous gaiety; and in winter, when the deep snows came, it wore a crown of white.

Inside the log house, a huge fireplace built of native rock formed a partition between the family sleeping quarters and a spacious room which served as living room, dining room, and kitchen. In winter, a large open fire of pine or cedar logs gave the house a fragrant, cheerful warmth. There was an iron cookstove in one corner and a wood box, always well filled.

Some of the stones in the fireplace showed the clear imprint of sea shells and small marine plants. Pat Garrett explained to his wife how they came to be there; how in ages past a great ocean had covered this land, even the tops of the mountains.

Now the sea had disappeared, but Eagle Creek remained, a clear little mountain stream flowing through their narrow green valley which was ringed about by forests of pine and spruce and distant mountain peaks.

By the time Elizabeth was three years old, she could make her way unerringly about the house and yard, using her hands skillfully to find her way. Instinctively, she learned to use the sense of smell, of taste or hearing, as well as the sense of touch to guide her. She was unaware of her handicap, and thought that everyone learned to "see" as she did.

She listened intently to the sighing of the wind in the pines, the birds calling to each other, and all the many sounds about her. She imitated the calls of the birds, just as she learned to imitate her mother's musical voice and to sing with her.

It soon became evident that the sightless little girl possessed a strong will and an adventurous spirit. Her dislike for being helped by the other children resulted in inevitable bumps and bruises, but with inate caution she avoided a repetition of unhappy experiences.

"See, Madrecita, how alert she is!" Mr. Garrett would say as they watched Elizabeth at play, eager and attentive, little body tense, ears straining for the sounds that would guide her in the darkness. "She is healthy and intelligent. We have much to be thankful for."

Mrs. Garrett was well aware of the effect his patient teaching had on Elizabeth's progress, as did Ida's loving care and guidance. She often thought that Ida was like a little mother herself, looking after the younger children so well. Yes, she had much to be thankful for.

One evening their father called to them from the corral. "Come up to the barn, children, I have something to show you."

"Hold my hand, Ida," Poe said as they started up the path. Poe didn't walk as well as his sisters. A few months before, he had been very ill with a severe fever which had left his arms and legs weakened and one leg twisted. It was hoped that his muscles would grow stronger with time. In later years his parents were told the fever was probably infantile paralysis.

"Don't hold *my* hand," Elizabeth said, running up the familiar path with sure feet.

"Come see what I have here," her father said. "It's a baby calf. He is too young to walk very well, so I carried him from the pasture." He put the calf down near the children, and it took a few wobbly steps.

Mr. Garrett placed Elizabeth's hands on the little animal's back. "See, here is his body. Feel his skin, so soft and warm, almost like fur. Now here are his legs, his neck, his head."

Her quick slender hands were busy, learning what a baby calf is like. Ida and Poe watched as their father taught Elizabeth to "see" with her sensitive hands.

"Now here is his mouth," Mr. Garrett said. "He has a strong mouth, so that he can get the milk he needs from his mother until he is old enough to eat grass. But like all babies, he likes milk. Now feel his ears. He can hear very well with those ears, especially when his mother calls him."

At that very moment a gentle "Moo-oo!"came from the barn.

"Supper is ready!" Mrs. Garrett called from the house, and they all laughed.

"We can't be late for Mama's good hot biscuits," Mr. Garrett said. He took the calf back to its mother, and gave the cow some hay. Then he lifted Poe up for a ride on his shoulder and they hurried into the house, with all three children trying to tell Mrs. Garrett about the new calf.

"Wait!" she laughed. "Please! Don't all talk at once."

"Madrecita is right," Mr. Garrett said. "Sit down, and we will tell her all about it, but one at a time."

After supper, while Ida helped with the dishes, Mr. Garrett sat in an easy chair with Poe on one knee and Elizabeth on the other. A cozy fire burned in the fireplace, as nights were cool in the mountain country, even in summer. This was the story hour, a favorite time.

"Why do you sometimes call Mama Madrecita?" Poe asked.

"Madrecita is Spanish for little mother," his father explained. "Your mother is of Spanish ancestry."

"What does that mean?" Poe persisted.

"That means her grandfather came to this country many

years ago from Spain, a country far away across the ocean. That is why we speak both Spanish and English in our family."

"Madrecita means little mother," Elizabeth nodded wisely.

"Where did your grandfather come from, Papa?" Ida had finished her work and sat on a stool near them.

"He lived in a southern state, a good many miles from here. When I was a boy, we lived on a big farm, called a plantation. I was sent to good schools and I studied hard. But after the Civil War my father died, and our land was sold."

"The Civil War?" Ida asked.

Mr. Garrett sighed. Ida should be in school; her curiosity and eagerness for learning were more apparent every day. He had taught her to read; she could recite most of the stories from the McGuffey First Reader by memory, she had read them so often. She could write and do simple sums too. But she was eight years old and growing fast, and there was no school within many miles of their ranch.

"You will learn about it in history class, when you go to school," he said. "It is too long a story to tell tonight, anyway."

"When did you come to our territory to live, Papa?" Ida persisted.

"Well, after our farm was sold, I was getting too old to go to school, and I needed a job. So I came west to Texas to work on a ranch, and for a time I was a Texas Ranger. Then I became an officer of the law in New Mexico here in Lincoln County where we now live."

"Tell us about it!" Poe's eyes brightened with interest. "Did you wear a badge, like John Poe wears?"

"Yes," Mr. Garrett smiled down at the eager little boy. "I was a sheriff just as John Poe is now, and the governor sent me with some other officers to arrest the outlaws in our territory."

"Tell us about the outlaws!" Poe demanded.

Mr. Garrett laughed. "Later, son. When you are older I will tell you more about those years. But not tonight."

Mrs. Garrett was listening quietly, thinking of those dangerous, troubled times. She had been only a young girl, living on her father's small ranch when she first heard of the handsome Texan who worked for neighboring ranchers in Lincoln County. It was after they were married that he was elected sheriff of the vast county.

"I am glad you are now a rancher and not an officer of the law," she spoke up. "But I am proud of the work you did, to make our territory safe. Yes, when the children are older, they must hear more about it. But now it is bedtime."

Later, when the children were asleep in their beds behind the stone fireplace wall, Mr. and Mrs. Garrett sat talking before the dying fire.

"I think we must soon leave this ranch, and find another place to live," he said. "Ida should be in school."

"But you worked so hard to build our house!" she protested. "And our beautiful fireplace! You are a very good teacher, why can you not teach the children at home? Remember, it was from you I learned to speak English."

Mr. Garrett smiled. She had learned English quickly, although her family had spoken only Spanish. He thought the accent she retained gave her careful English an added charm.

"I had an apt pupil, Madrecita. You learned very quickly. But there are many things I can't teach the children, and even if I could, the work of the ranch takes most of my time. And there is another reason why we should move. Elizabeth needs more freedom to get about alone. The mountain country is too rugged for a child who can't see. I think a place in the Rio Grande valley south of here, or in the Pecos River valley to the southeast, would be ideal. There is water for irrigation in either valley and we could grow our own fruit and vegetables, as well as feed for our livestock. We should have a small ranch and farm combined. The land is open and level, and Elizabeth could run and play and learn to ride. It would be easier for Poe to get about, too."

"And there would be a school?"

He nodded. "We would be sure to get a place near a town with schools. The children could learn much from living on a farm, too."

"Will we be near El Paso?" she asked wistfully. She had never been to El Paso, Texas, the only large city in the Southwest, although it was very near the southern border of New Mexico. She had heard fascinating stories about the fine stores and hotels and restaurants there.

"It wouldn't be too far; I think we could visit El Paso some day," her husband promised.

Before a month had passed, Mr. Garrett had made arrangements for the move.

"First we will go to Las Cruces," he told Madrecita, as the children listened, wide-eyed and curious. "I have friends there. We will live there while I look for our farm. We should reach Las Cruces in four or five days."

"How will we go?" Poe asked.

"By covered wagon, just like the pioneers traveled when the

18

first settlers came to this country. We will take only what we need, clothing and bedding and a few cooking utensils. After we are located, I will come back for our furniture."

"Where will we sleep?"

"Sometimes we may stop at the home of friends, but usually we will camp near a stream or a well. We will cook our meals over a campfire and sleep in our wagon."

Ida and Poe danced with joy, and three year old Elizabeth was caught up in their excitement, although she was not fully aware of the changes taking place.

The Studebaker wagon looked almost new with a fresh coat of dark blue paint on side boards and wheel spokes. Curving wooden bows arched above the wagon bed, fastened at each side, with a new white canvas cover stretched over, providing shelter from rain or too much sun. On this fine morning the canvas was rolled up high to allow a good view of the country.

A homemade pine chest was fastened to the side of the wagon, holding a few pots and pans and a supply of bacon, potatoes, flour, coffee, beans and dried fruit. Two metal trunks held the family's clothing and were placed inside the wagon, along with several fat rolls of bedding.

Two of Mr. Garrett's best mares were hitched to the wagon. His favorite riding horse, Scout, would follow along behind, led by a rope attached to the end-gate.

"All aboard now! We're ready to go!" Mr. Garrett helped Ida and Poe as they climbed up, squealing with delight at the sight of the secluded canvas-roofed interior. The cover was higher than their heads, and there was room to walk about between the trunks and bed rolls. It was like a little house of their own.

"You can sit on the bedding," their father said, "and sometimes take turns riding up front on the seat with Mama and me."

"Where is Elizabeth?" Mrs. Garrett placed a last bundle of clothing in the wagon.

In the confusion no one had noticed that Elizabeth hadn't followed the others as usual. Then they saw her, standing alone and very close to the familiar back steps of the log house. Frustration and bewilderment were plainly written on the little face as she waited, tense and alert, straining to understand what was happening.

"Come, Elizabeth, you must see how we will be traveling." Mr. Garrett took her hand and led her to the wagon. Their departure was delayed as he patiently helped her to explore and "see" in her own way the covered wagon that would be their home for the next few days.

19

At last they were on their way. Sitting beside her husband on the high spring seat, Mrs. Garrett looked back at the picturesque log house. Tears that had threatened all morning wet her cheeks. She had been secure and happy in that house, after the turbulent first months of their marriage when her bridegroom had held the hazardous office of sheriff. What would the future hold for them now?

Her quiet tears were not unnoticed by her husband. "Never mind, Madrecita," he said gently, "we will have another house, maybe even better than this one."

"I am sorry, my Pat." She wiped her eyes. "Yes, I know we will have another house. We will make another home." But she knew there could be no better or happier home than the one they were leaving.

The closest settlement to their ranch was Lincoln Town, a good day's drive away. Mr. Garrett said they might spend the night there, if Madrecita wished. Lincoln had two hotels.

The sun was going down behind the pine-covered mountains when they drove into Lincoln. Buckboards, saddle horses and pedestrians crowded the narrow main street. Court was in session! During terms of court judges, lawyers, witnesses and spectators poured into the county seat from all parts of the territory, filling the hotels and any spare rooms available in private homes.

"Well, we can't get rooms here tonight, that's sure," Mr. Garrett said. "We'll drive on through town, and make camp on the Bonito."

Mrs. Garrett was secretly pleased. She would much prefer camping by that lovely mountain stream. Lincoln Town held too many disturbing memories.

"What is that large building, Papa?" Ida asked, as they drove slowly down the crowded winding street.

"That is the county courthouse," he explained. "One of the upstairs rooms was my office when I was sheriff."

"I want to see! Let me see!" Elizabeth demanded.

"Not now, little one. Some day, maybe, you children should visit that building. A lot of history has been made there."

Elizabeth frowned, disconcerted as she had been all day by conversation she couldn't understand. Repeatedly, Poe and Ida had exclaimed over things she was unable to "see". It was much better at home, she thought, where she could see right away!

Mrs. Garrett felt relief that court was in session. If the place had been less crowded, Mr. Garrett might have been tempted to stop to visit the courthouse again.

How well she knew that building, with its solid, adobe walls, more than two feet thick on the lower story, its high ceilings, narrow windows, and many corner fireplaces for heating. The Garretts' living quarters as well as the Sheriff's office had been on the upper floor.

The lower floor held a large courtroom and several other county offices, as well as rooms for visitors. But the guard room, armory and jail were on the upper floor, uncomfortably close the Garretts' rooms. Often prisoners were dangerous, violent men. One of these was the notorious young outlaw, William Bonney, known throughout the territory as Billy the Kid.

The building looked just the same, although conditions had changed greatly for the good in the few years that had elapsed. Billy the Kid and other outlaw leaders had been killed or captured, and ranchers were able to operate without constant harassment. There were the outside stairs leading down from the jail. Billy had escaped from jail for the last time and had fled down those stairs, after brutally murdering two unsuspecting guards. The escape had led inevitably to the outlaw's death soon after.

Mrs. Garrett shuddered. No, they should not stop to sleep in Lincoln Town with its reminders of those anxious times. And she hoped it would be many years before the children would of necessity learn about that era, which had become a vital part of New Mexico's history. They were certainly too young to hear of it now!

They drove on through town, past the hotels, the two general stores, the old *Torreon*, once a refuge from Indian attacks, past the trading post where Indians now traded peaceably with their white neighbors, and the Catholic Church and cemetery, the *camposanto*.

The sun was low when they reached the open meadows that bordered Bonito Creek. "This is a good place to spend the night," Mr. Garrett said, helping the children down by the clear tumbling stream.

"Oh, how pretty!" Ida exclaimed. "*Muy bonito!* Now I know how it got its name!" The valley was carpeted with lush green grass dotted with a gay profusion of color; bluebells and white anemones, red and yellow pentstemon, purple verbena, crimson Indian paint brush, the delicate lavendar phlox—every color and variety of wild flower abounded.

The children ran about, releasing their pent-up energy, while Mr. Garrett built a campfire and cared for the horses. Mrs. Garrett opened the pine chest and started supper. The inviting smell of bacon frying soon brought the children back to the camp.

Later, they spread their bed rolls in the wagon and went to bed, warm and snug, in spite of the crispness of the mountain air. Ida looked out at the bright stars, which seemed to hang just above the dark mountain top. "I wish Elizabeth could see the stars," she thought sleepily.

Chapter   2

CHAPTER 2

Next day the road dropped from the high mountain country into a broad valley. Far away across the valley lay a long expanse of shimmering white, and beyond that, another lower range of mountains.

Ida was puzzled. "How can there be so much snow, Papa, when the weather is warm?"

"Let me see the snow!" Elizabeth demanded.

"It isn't snow, " their father explained. "It's called the White Sands, although it's really not sand at all, but miles and miles of pure white gypsum. Another thing to learn about when you go to school."

Elizabeth fidgeted impatiently. "Let me see!" she repeated.

"Just wait, little one," Mr. Garrett said. "We will camp there tonight, and you will all have a chance to examine it. Then you will see the white sand."

The road now led across the wide, dry Tularosa basin where the only vegetation was sagebrush and greasewood. The desert air grew warm, but the wagon cover provided welcome protection from the hot sun. It was late afternoon when the road at last skirted the rolling banks of white that looked so much like snow.

They made camp in the shelter of a mountainous dune, and the children began their explorations.

"It isn't snow, it's warm!" Poe shouted. The sand was soft but firm, and they ran up and down the dunes, climbing to the top and rolling down again, shrieking with pleasure. When they grew tired, they sat down and dug tunnels and caves. The sand was cool and damp under the surface.

"It feels like sugar," Elizabeth said, tasting a sample which she immediately spat out, "but it isn't sugar."

"Papa says it is gypsum," Ida explained again. "Anyway, it's fun to play on." And play they did, until it was growing dark and Mrs. Garrett called them to supper. Then they spread their beds on the soft white sand and slept under the stars. This was the most fun of all!

The children were reluctant to leave next morning, but they climbed into the wagon and the horses were directed toward Las Cruces in another valley beyond the Organ Mountains and still two days away.

Las Cruces was a small settlement with green gardens and trees, a welcome sight after the semidesert country they had crossed. Mr. Garrett rented a house for the family to live in while he made several trips about the country, looking for the farm he wished to buy.

There was another reason for their stay in Las Cruces. A few weeks after they arrived there, a fourth child was born to the Garretts, a lovely little girl who was promptly named Anne. Sometimes Mr. Garrett was away for several days, but the neighbors were kind and friendly. Mrs. Garrett was glad to find that many of them were Spanish speaking, like her own family.

The house was cool and comfortable, built of brown *adobe* as most of the houses were, a kind of brick made of mud and straw and dried in the hot sun. The yard was shaded by a big cottonwood tree.

A large canal, called the *acequia madre* or mother ditch ran through the town, carrying water from the nearby river, the Rio Grande. Water was diverted from the main canal into smaller irrigation ditches to water the lawns and gardens.

Mrs. Garrett was alarmed to find the big canal very close to their house. The water was deep and swift.

"You must not play near the *acequia*," she told the children, "It is dangerous."

Elizabeth was not yet four years old. She liked the sound of running water, it made her think of Eagle Creek where she had often gone wading with Poe and Ida. Why should she be afraid of the water?

One morning Mrs. Garrett heard a shriek and a splash from the direction of the canal. She ran to the door, followed by Ida. Poe was pointing to the canal and crying: "Lisbeth fell in the water! Hurry, Mama!"

Mrs. Garrett was almost paralyzed with fright. She could not swim! As she ran toward the canal she saw a young man jump from a bicycle and leap into the water. He reached the struggling little girl quickly and pulled her up onto the bank.

"*Gracias! Gracias!* Oh, thank you!" Mrs. Garrett cried.

"It was nothing, Ma'am; but I'm glad that I happened to be riding this way." He carried the dripping Elizabeth into the house, where they soon made sure she had not been harmed by the water.

They learned that the young man's name was Will Robinson. A reporter for the local newspaper, barely out of his teens, he had come to New Mexico from the east for his health and had a room down the street.

"The doctors say this warm sunny climate will help my cough," he said. "I ride this way often on my bicycle, but I didn't expect to go fishing today!"

Mr. Garrett heard about the incident when he came home that night.

"Tomorrow I will see that young man, and tell him again how grateful we are," he said. "You were lucky to have such a friend, Elizabeth. He saved your life, little one."

"I won't play near the canal again," she promised. "I don't like to be a fish! I got water in my nose."

"We will be moving soon, anyway," Mr. Garrett said. "I have the farm we have been looking for. It is in the Pecos Valley nearly two hundred miles east of here."

The Studebaker wagon topped a gentle rise, and a wide expanse of green farmland lay before them.

"There is our farm," Mr. Garrett said. They could see a house near a grove of trees with a barn and corral nearby.

Mrs. Garrett looked pleased. "Such a large house! Two stories."

"Well, bigger than our log house," he agreed, "and I like the white stucco finish. There's a good orchard back of the house, and that green field is alfalfa. We will have plenty of hay for our livestock."

Elizabeth flexed her slender fingers. Why did the others "see" certain objects before she was able to! "I want to see the house, Papa! And the barn!"

"Soon, little one. Soon you will see everything. Whoa! Here we are!"

The horses stopped readily. It had been a long trip from Las Cruces to Roswell; more than a week on the road this time. The children started to climb down, eager to begin their explorations.

"Wait!" Mrs. Garrett said suddenly. "Look, Pat! The *acequia!* You bought a farm with an *acequia!*"

"Of course, Madrecita. We can't have a garden or flowers or an orchard without irrigation water."

There it was, a deep irrigation canal running past the grassy yard. A narrow foot-bridge was the only means of crossing between the house and the barn.

"But it is too dangerous, for Elizabeth, for Poe . . ." she said in dismay, "and so close to the house!"

"That is unfortunate, but the children must learn about danger," Mr. Garrett said calmly. "Come, Elizabeth, you will be first. The rest of you wait where you are."

He lifted the little girl from the wagon and led her down the sloping bank of the canal.

"Listen to the sound of the water," he said. "This water is not like Eagle Creek; it is deep and swift and not to play in. But there is a bridge, and you can learn to cross it safely. Come, I will show you."

They climbed up the bank and he led her to the bridge. "Kneel down here, Elizabeth. See, it is just so wide." He guided her groping hands to measure the distance. "Now we will cross together. There is just room for us both if we walk carefully." He took her hand and they crossed to the other side.

"Now I will walk back, and you will follow, walking in the middle of the bridge behind me. Measure first, think carefully, listen, and walk straight."

She knelt again and took the measure of the boards. Then she stood up and walked across behind her father, intent, listening, slender bare feet cautiously finding the way.

"Good girl! Now you may cross alone."

Slowly at first, then with increasing confidence she repeated the feat several times.

"Now you can cross safely anytime if you are careful," her father said. "Come, Poe, it's your turn."

"Come, Poe, and see the bridge," Elizabeth said, "but be careful!"

Mrs. Garrett smiled, but she felt a twinge of sadness as she watched Poe awkwardly crossing the bridge. Perhaps his frail limbs would grow stronger here in the warm sunshine where there was more freedom for play and exercise.

Ida took Elizabeth's hand. "Now we will see the yard. Come, Poe." They ran about on the soft grass, happy to use their cramped muscles. And as Mr. Garrett took the baby and helped his wife down from the wagon, he was glad to see that she was smiling, her fear of the *acequia* forgotten.

One morning late in the summer, Mrs. Garrett watched from the kitchen window as the children played outside. They had placed a sturdy ladder against a low, flat-roofed shed next to the barn and were playing Follow the Leader, a favorite game. She watched as Ida led the way, calling her instructions to the others. Elizabeth was next. Sometimes it seemed that she could see as well as anyone; with her sharp sense of hearing and her skillful hands and nimble feet she kept up with Ida amazingly well. Feeling expertly for the rungs of the ladder, she climbed up like an agile little squirrel and began taking her careful measurements of the roof. Poe followed with slow determination. Mrs. Garrett sighed. He *was* getting stronger; the farm was a good place for all of them. Turning to the cradle where the new baby Anne cooed and smiled at her mother, she breathed a prayer of thanksgiving for the new home, for Poe's gift of sight, and that Elizabeth, who was denied that gift, was endowed with a healthy, active body.

Every day the children explored the orchard, the corral, and the big shadowy barn. They climbed over bales of sweet-smelling hay, found hidden hen's nests, and gathered newly-laid eggs for next morning's breakfast.

The animals were Elizabeth's special delight: the colts and calves, the dog and puppies, the cat and kittens, the baby chicks and downy ducks. She learned to "see" her furry and feathery friends with her eager fingers. She imitated the sounds they made and fed and petted them and sang to them.

She liked the feeling of high places and had no knowledge of fear. Scaling the ladder to the shed roof, the stacks of hay in the barn, or climbing the trees with limbs low enough for her reaching arms were everyday occurrences.

A large old apple tree with low, spreading branches became her private haven. Autumn was coming to the valley, and the spicy scent of ripening apples filled the air. She spent many happy hours high in the tree, making up little songs about the sunshine and the breeze that rocked the boughs with a swaying motion.

Mr. Garrett bought a gentle pony, and the children rode him bareback with a rope around his neck to guide him. Ida showed Elizabeth how to hold onto his mane and scramble up on his back without help, but Poe couldn't quite make it. When it was his turn to ride, Ida led "Old Pony" to a broad tree stump and sturdy Elizabeth lifted the little boy bodily onto the stump. Then, by gripping the patient animal's mane and, aided by a mighty push from Elizabeth, Poe achieved his seat.

Sometimes Elizabeth rode with her father on his horse, Scout, as he made trips about the farm.

"Tell me where we are," he said one day as she sat behind him, holding lightly to his belt. Her well-trained ears and keen sense of smell gave her the clues she needed. The sound of Scout's hooves told her whether they were riding on grass of bare ground or rocky soil, and the whinny of the pony, the bark of Bouncer, the dog, the cackle of the chickens, or the different barnyard smells would tell her when they were near the barn. But now the steady hum of bees and the fragrance of alfalfa blossoms told her they were near the field.

"The alfalfa field! Why are there so many bees, Papa?"

"They are busy gathering honey from the blossoms. Let's stop awhile." They dismounted and sat in the shade of a tree.

"Open your hand now, and keep very still." He placed a few purple blossoms in her hand. Soon a bee buzzed down and lit on the flowers. For a few seconds it searched busily for the sweet nectar inside, then buzzed away.

"Where does he go now?" she asked.

"He flies away and stores the honey somewhere, perhaps in a hollow tree. Soon we will have our own honey. I am building storehouses called hives for the bees in the orchard. Now let's ride back to the barn, I have something to show you."

In the barnyard Mr. Garrett placed Elizabeth's hands on an unsteady, fuzzy little animal. "It's a new baby colt. How would you like him for your own?"

Her face glowed with pleasure as her quick hands went over the colt, finding his soft, furry body, his slender legs, and his head and ears and mouth. "He is beautiful! He will be my own pony!"

"Yes, you may care for him and feed him when he is older. And name him whatever you wish."

"His name is Trotter," she said.

The months flew by. Anne was no longer a baby, but an active little girl who followed Elizabeth and Poe about or sat with them under the apple tree listening to their stories and songs. Elizabeth rode Trotter for hours on end, with Poe often following on Old Pony, now his sole property. Ida was old enough to ride a regular saddle horse to school each day. What fascinating stories she had to tell!

"I want to go to school, too," Elizabeth said more and more often.

When spring came, she loved her apple tree more than ever. The fragrance of the delicate apple blossoms enchanted her as she sat high in the branches with the warm breeze gently touching her face. Birds sang and called to each other, sometimes flying so close she could hear the faint whirring sound of their wings. How wonderful it would be to fly! She made up new songs about the sweet apple blossoms and the birds. She sang constantly in a pure true voice.

"Elizabeth has musical talent," Mr. Garrett said to his wife one day. "She seems to have inherited your ear for music and your singing voice. She really should have musical training."

Elizabeth overheard. She wasn't sure what was meant by musical talent, but she knew she liked to sing with Madrecita, especially the melodious Spanish songs her mother taught her. Mr. Garrett didn't sing, but she liked his pleasant voice, too, when he told the children stories.

Her favorite story was about the brave explorer, Columbus, who sailed across a strange ocean to find an unknown land. One day her father made three small wooden boats, and with Ida's help, equipped them with sails.

"Now we have the *Nina*, the *Pinta*, and the *Santa Maria*,"

Ida said, as they launched the boats on the duck pond. With the aid of long willow sticks they spent much time guiding their valiant craft across the stormy Atlantic. Elizabeth's role as Columbus was taken for granted; Ida was Queen Isabella, and Poe an obliging little King Ferdinand.

"We can't put it off much longer," Mr. Garrett told his wife one day. "Elizabeth must be told that she is blind. I have investigated; there is a fine school for the blind in Austin, Texas. The children who are enrolled at an early age make the best progress. We should send her there soon."

"But she is so little, so young to be away from us," Mrs. Garrett said. "How can we let her go?"

"Of course we will miss her, Madrecita. It will not be easy for her or for us. But she has courage and intelligence. She likes to learn, and in a little while she will be busy and happy at school with so many new experiences opening up for her. And she must receive a good education. She must!"

Elizabeth sat in the orchard, listening to the sounds about her. She could hear the busy hum of her little friends, the honeymakers. She heard the whinny of Trotter, her own pony, in the pasture nearby, and the cackle of a hen announcing a newly-laid egg in the barn. Somewhere a dog barked, and her own dog, Bouncer, answered. A warm breeze touched her face. How beautiful the world seemed!

She jumped to her feet when she heard familiar footsteps. Perhaps her father would have time to sit with her and tell her one of his stories.

"What are you doing, Elizabeth?" he asked, as he drew her down on the grass beside him.

"I am listening to all the beautiful sounds, Papa. And feel, the wind is so soft, and it brings the smell of the roses."

"Yes, so many sounds, and each is different. The bees make one kind, the birds another; the voices of your family, all different. Just as you, little one, are different."

"How am I different, Papa?"

He took her hands and laid one on each of her eyes.

"The other children have eyes, too," he said, "and yet your eyes are different. They see with their eyes, but you see with your hands, your fingers."

"How can they see with their eyes?"

"Their eyes tell them many things your fingers tell you. They see the bridge over the *acequia* without touching it. They know where Trotter is grazing, or where Bouncer is running. They see them, with their eyes, although they may not be near enough to touch."

She struggled to comprehend this startling knowledge, a puzzled frown on her face. Was this the reason she often had to wait to see and the others didn't?

"They learn to read with their eyes," her father continued, "but you will learn to read with your fingers."

"I want to see with my eyes, too" she said eagerly. "Can't I see with my eyes, Papa?"

"No, little one, you can't; your eyes are different. But there are other children, like you, who can't see in the usual way. And you can learn to do many things, without your eyes. How would you like to make a trip with me soon?"

"A trip! In the covered wagon?" she clapped her hands with pleasure.

"No, a trip by train. First we will go to El Paso on the stage-coach. Then we will ride on a train to another city called Austin. In Austin there is a fine school for children who see as you do. Children who see with their eyes can go to any school, but this school is special, just as you are special."

"Will Ida go? And Poe?"

"No, they will stay here with Madrecita and Anne, but I will go with you."

"Will you stay with me at the school?" she asked anxiously.

"I will stay for a while, until you are ready for me to come home. Then you will be with the other children and the teachers, until time to come home for Christmas vacation. You will enjoy school. The teachers will read many wonderful stories to you, more than I have time to read. And best of all, they will teach you to read stories yourself, by using your fingers."

She frowned. How could she read with her fingers?

"Tell me more about the school," she demanded.

"Well, you will make many new friends there. There is a big yard where you will play with the other children. And you will not only learn to read, you will sing and dance and learn to play the piano."

"A piano!" she clapped her hands. They had once visited a family in Roswell who had a piano; she remembered the lovely tinkling notes that came from this strange instrument. She would like to play the piano! But something her father had said disturbed her: "You will be with the other children and the teachers . . ." She would be away from home, from Madrecita!

"I don't want to go, Papa. I would like better to stay here," she announced firmly.

"You *must* go, little one. You must believe that I know what is best for you. You have always liked the story of Columbus who sailed across a great ocean. No one knew much about that ocean, and many people were afraid of it, but Columbus was brave, and he kept on going until he found a new land.

"The school will be strange to you at first, but I know you will be brave, too." He took her restless little hands in his. "Just think! Some day these hands will play the piano! Yes, you must go. Remember, I am going with you on the train to Austin."

Her spirits rose at the alluring thought of a train ride with her father, and an inviting school where children could play the piano! Anyway, Papa said she must go. Her trust in him was complete and unwavering.

"When can we go, Papa? I want to see my school!"

"The school term begins next month," he said. "Now we will start planning our trip."

"All finished at last!" Mrs. Garrett said. For days she had been sewing, making school clothes. Now there were four new dresses for Ida, four for Elizabeth, and four shirts for Poe laid out on their beds.

"Let me see them! Let me see my dresses!" Elizabeth begged. Her mother placed a crisp new dress in her hands.

"This is a blue one, blue like the summer sky. You can tell it from the others because it has small buttons. Now this one is yellow, like yellow sunshine, or the yellow roses in our yard. Its buttons are medium size." Elizabeth's fingers were busily memorizing the buttons. "And this dress is red, like fire, warm and bright. It has larger buttons. *This* one is a party dress, with lace and pink ribbons. It looks like apple blossoms, soft and white."

"Will I go to a party?" she was fairly dancing with excitement.

"Sometime, yes." Mama promised.

Elizabeth had new shoes, too, that squeaked a little when she tried them, and a warm coat and scarf and hat to take with her for the cooler weather which would come later. The coat was green, Mama told her, like the green alfalfa.

At last everything was ready, and one morning Mr. Garrett and Elizabeth boarded the stagecoach which took passengers and mail from Roswell to El Paso. The other children waved and shouted goodbyes, and Madrecita waved and wiped her eyes as they drove away. The trip to Austin had begun.

Chapter 3

CHAPTER 3

The railroad station was hot and noisy. Outside a medley of shrill voices, clanging bells, and the chuff-chuff of the coal-burning engine made Elizabeth's head ache. She tightened her grip on her father's hand as he helped her up the steps of the train and into the day coach, then down a narrow aisle between rows of double seats.

"Here is a good seat for us, next to the window," he said, placing their suitcases in a rack overhead and opening the window for fresh air. He closed it again, however, as coal smoke from the big engine swept in, making their eyes burn.

Elizabeth's groping hands moved swiftly, exploring the plush covered seats. "The cushions are red, like your new dress with the large buttons," Mr. Garrett said. But even thinking of the new red dress didn't make her feel better. The warm air smelled musty and strange. This trip was not fun at all, so uncomfortable and terrifying! If she were only at home, this very moment, sitting in her apple tree, with the cool, sweet-scented breeze blowing from the alfalfa field! She thought of her mother and baby Anne. What were Ida and Poe and Trotter and Bouncer and all the happy animals doing now? When would she see them again? Two big tears rolled down her cheeks.

The car began to move. "We're on our way, *querida*." Mr. Garrett wiped the tears away gently. "You are starting a new, exciting adventure." *Querida*, dear one! He often called Mama *querida*. The ache in her chest lessened as he went on talking calmly of the things she would see and do at school.

"Now rest your head against me for a while, and close your eyes. I will tell you about the country we are passing through. I see cattle grazing in a pasture and a horse with a colt standing under a tree. The trees are small here, but there will be many big trees in Austin."

"Like my apple tree?"

"Yes, little one." How soothing his voice was! The wheels of the railroad car were going clickety-clack, clickety-clack. She fell asleep and dreamed she was swinging on a bough of her tree. When she awoke hours later her father told her Austin was only a half hour away! Cushioned comfortably by pillows supplied by the friendly conductor, the tired little girl had slept through her first night away from home!

"We will soon see your school," Mr. Garrett said as he washed her face and smoothed her dark curls, "your school that will some day give you a diploma."

"Diploma, diploma," she repeated, rested and smiling now. "Some day I will have a diploma!"

Mr. Piner, the superintendent of the school, met them at the train. Elizabeth liked his pleasant voice; it was almost as nice as her father's.

"We are very glad you have come here, Elizabeth," he said as he took her hand. "We have many happy children in our school who will soon be your friends. I will take you there now, and you and your father will meet the teachers. Then I will show you both through the buildings and around the grounds."

"Thank you," she said politely. "I have come to get my diploma."

"Good! I am certain you will get your diploma," Mr. Piner assured her, as they walked to his waiting carriage.

The school was located on the outskirts of Austin, away from the noise and confusion of the city. Holding her father's hand, Elizabeth first met the teachers, the cook, and other helpers. She listened intently to each name, and to the voice that went with the name. A tour of the class rooms, sleeping rooms, dining room and kitchen followed.

"Now this is the main hall, where we assemble for games, music, singing—all kinds of programs," Mr. Piner said. "We have one piano here; there are others in the practice rooms."

"A piano! Please, may I see the piano?" Her hands brushed eagerly over the keyboard. "I am going to learn to play the piano. Oh, I love my school, Papa! I am very glad we came to Austin!"

The dormitory for smaller girls held twelve junior size beds. Other children would be arriving next day, but Elizabeth slept alone in the big room that night, in the narrow bed assigned to her. It seemed strange and lonely not to share a soft bed with Ida or Anne, but she knew her father was near, in a room reserved for visiting parents with the door open between his room and hers.

The sheets had a strange smell, a little like the disinfectant Mr. Garrett kept in the barn for treating cuts the horses sometimes received from barbed wire fences. At home, the sheets smelled fresh and clean, after Madrecita had washed them and dried them in sunshine and fresh air. However, the unusual activities of the day had tired her, and she fell asleep quickly.

Next morning, Elizabeth and her father went through the rooms again and again. Patiently he helped her to "see" the desks, chairs, and other furnishings in different rooms; to locate doors and halls; to learn the exact location of her bed in relation to her small clothes closet and the adjoining bathroom.

"You will be able to find your way about without help in a few days," Mr. Garrett said with satisfaction, "and of course after I leave other children will guide you when you need them, the children who have been here longer."

"Please do not leave, Papa," she begged anxiously.

"Well, not yet, *querida*. Not until you tell me I can go."

In the afternoon they explored the play area. A large, grassy yard was safely enclosed by a sturdy mesh fence. With Mr. Garrett's help, she located the swings, slides, and bars for climbing. They found several large shade trees, and Elizabeth began to search for low branches, but found none she could touch. How could she ever climb such trees!

Then, just outside the dining room window, she discovered a large pecan tree with low, spreading boughs.

"I can climb this one!" she exclaimed happily, reaching eagerly for a sturdy limb.

"Not yet!" her father cautioned. "We must ask permission first. It may be against the rules to climb trees here."

At least I can sit under this tree, she thought, and soon I will ask permission to climb it.

Several days went by. Other children arrived, and those who had been at the school before helped new students and their parents to become familiar with their surroundings. As Elizabeth would learn later, some of the children had partial vision, which enabled them to act as guides for the totally blind.

Physical training was included for all students, beginning with simple sitting-up exercises, rope jumping, and folk dancing; which would progress to skating, swimming, and all kinds of playground games as the children developed confidence and physical endurance.

At first the smaller children spent much time in the play area. Elizabeth liked the challenge of finding the swings, slides and bars without assistance. Accustomed as she was to outdoor play, climbing, and horseback riding, she entered into any physical activity with zest. She had always liked the feel of high places; the caress of the wind high above the ground filled her with joy.

Classes were beginning too, and the days were divided into periods with programs designed for different age groups. The music period was a happy time for the smaller children. A teacher played the piano and taught them simple tunes and nursery rhymes set to music. Singing was familiar ground for Elizabeth, but the music of the piano suddenly opened a whole new exciting world.

"I think it is time for me to go home," Mr. Garrett said one morning. "I must see about Madrecita and the other children, you know, and it is time to cut the hay so Trotter will have his winter feed."

Elizabeth was appalled!

"Oh, Papa, please don't go so soon! Can't someone cut the hay, so that you can stay with me?"

"No, little one, I can't do that."

"Then let me go home with you," she pleaded.

"No, you can't do that either. You must be a brave girl, as you promised me." He took her hands in his. "Sometimes you will wish for home, but you must remember the other children are away from their parents, too, but they will stay. You will be busy, learning many things, and in a few weeks I will come back to take you home for Christmas. Perhaps by that time you can play a tune on the piano for me. These hands of yours have much to learn."

She was silent, trying to imagine how it would be without her father. She knew her way about the school rooms and play yard, and she could find her chair and table in the classroom and her place in the dining room. She could go without help to her own closet and bed in the dormitory. Some of the children were already her friends. And the thought of learning to play the piano cheered her. She took a deep breath.

"Yes, Papa, I think you can leave me now," she said.

"Good! I knew you would not disappoint me. Remember, you are like Columbus, exploring a whole new world!" He drew her to him briefly. "Now I hear the dinner gong. Go along into the dining room and I will be on my way." He kissed her and hurried away.

She walked slowly into the dining room. She was determined not to cry. Columbus didn't cry!

She sat at her table with other young children. Usually she was hungry at mealtime, but now she was sure the lump in her throat would not allow her to swallow if she tried to eat. She knew the food was there, specially prepared and cut in bite-sized portions for easy handling, and she could smell the enticing odors. She took one bite but her appetite had left her completely.

"Eat your lunch, Elizabeth," a voice said. "You must eat your lunch."

The voice sounded strange and harsh to the homesick child. Suddenly she slipped from her chair, groped deftly about to get her direction, and ran to the door. Before the startled teacher could move she was outside, her searching hands reaching for the low branches of the pecan tree. In a flash, she had climbed high up in its branches.

"Come down, Elizabeth! Come down at once!" stern voices

commanded, then coaxed, but to no avail.

"I will send for Mr. Garrett," she heard the supervisor say. "I am sure his train hasn't left yet."

Let them call my father, the rebellious little girl thought. He will understand! And maybe he will take me home with him. But she knew differently when he came striding into the yard a few minutes later. She thought even his footsteps sounded angry!

"Come down at once, Elizabeth!" the dear familiar voice commanded sternly. "You have disappointed me!"

She had been taught to obey that voice without question. She slid down into his arms and burst into tears.

"I'm sorry, Papa," she sobbed. "I *meant* to be brave."

"Of course you did, little one." He wiped the tears gently from the sightless brown eyes. "Now tell the ladies you are sorry for the trouble you caused them. Perhaps when you have been here longer you will be permitted to climb this tree again."

Apologies were made, and the supervisor agreed that Elizabeth could climb the tree at times, since her father approved.

"Now I know you won't let me down, *querida*," he said, taking her aside. "Time passes quickly. Next month you will receive a surprise, a package for your birthday. And remember, in only a few weeks I will come back to take you home for Christmas."

"You'd better go before your train leaves," she agreed, her composure restored. For the second time, her father bade her goodbye and hurried away.

The chastened little girl returned to the dining room with her teacher. The food tasted much better now.

In December, Mr. Garrett came a day early to attend a program the children were giving. There were Christmas carols and a pageant and several piano selections, with many students taking part. The school provided and encouraged musical training for all who had even a slight interest or talent for it. But the number Mr. Garrett enjoyed most was a jolly little tune played by six year old Elizabeth. His heart was warmed by the glow of sheer pleasure reflected in her face. Perhaps his fervent wish for this child's security and happiness could be realized. Would music be the key which would open the door to Elizabeth's future?

Next day they were on the train again. The little girl was fairly bursting with excitement, there was so much to tell Madrecita and the others! She would tell them all about her wonderful school where she was learning to play the piano, and that soon she would learn to read with her fingers in a special kind of book called Braille!

The house was filled with the smell of apples and oranges, of mince pie and cookies, and a turkey roasting in the oven.

"Come see the tree!" Poe tugged at Elizabeth. "I helped Ida decorate the tree."

A rancher friend had brought the little evergreen tree from their old home in the mountains. How good it smelled! It brought back dim memories of Eagle Creek, the sound of the running water, and the scent of the pine forests. Her hands moved over the tree and the decorations of paper chains and strings of popcorn. And beneath the tree, she discovered several mysterious packages wrapped and tied with bows of ribbon.

She went from room to room, fondly touching remembered objects and enjoying the delicious aroma of Madrecita's cooking. Then she went out with Ida and Poe to see her pets, not forgetting to take a lump of sugar for Trotter, who seemed to be waiting for her at the corral gate.

When Ida and Poe went back to the house, she lingered at the corral, talking softly to Trotter: "Tomorrow we will take a ride," she told him. Just then a soft whinny and stamping told her another horse was near.

One of Mr. Garrett's ranch hands had stopped by a few minutes earlier, leaving his horse standing near the stump where Poe had often mounted Old Pony. The men had walked down to the field to discuss some needed work.

Elizabeth went over to the horse and patted his shoulder. It had been months since she had been on a horse, and the urge was irresistible. She climbed on the stump, reached for the saddle horn and with one sure leap mounted the horse. Startled by this unfamiliar little creature on his back, the excited animal bolted down the road toward the field with the reins flying in the air! Elizabeth hung on doggedly until the horse came to a stop near a tree, a short distance from where the two men stood rooted to the spot. Then she slid from the saddle, found the tree, and promptly sat down with her back to the trunk, waiting. She wasn't surprised that her father came to her at once. Papa was always there when she needed him!

"I knew you would find me," she said calmly.

"Well, it wasn't hard, as it happened the horse brought you straight to us." His tone told her he was displeased with her! "That was a foolish thing you did. Even older people hesitate to mount a strange horse. You might have been thrown and badly hurt. Remember, Elizabeth, before you do something, first *think*. Be sure of what you are doing, *then* go ahead."

Elizabeth was dismayed. She had disappointed Papa again!

"You are right, Papa. I didn't use my head that time," she agreed penitently.

How quickly the days went by! Suddenly it was time to pack her suitcase again for the trip back to Austin. This time, however, the pangs of leaving were lessened by the knowledge that she would be coming home again in a few months to spend the summer. And now she could hardly wait to get back to the school and the many exciting things that happened there.

"You are going to learn to read," a teacher announced one morning. "After a while, you will be able to read stories from books called Braille, just as your parents or teachers read other books. You will learn to read with your fingertips."

Elizabeth listened, spellbound, flexing her restless, delicate fingers. From that moment, another world of wonders began to unfold.

Even the youngest children were started in Braille classes. The fingers must be sensitive to distinguish the intricate characters, which are formed by a series of raised dots to represent the letters of the alphabet. Younger children found it easier than older students attempting it for the first time.

Music lessons, Braille lessons! The world was filled with wonders! As her father had predicted, Elizabeth was now too busy to be homesick. She spent many happy hours alone in the practice room, playing and singing tunes of her own.

"Elizabeth has a gift not possessed by all who love music," her teacher wrote Mr. Garrett, "she has a perfect ear."

When the weather was good, and classes over for the day, her little friends would gather about her, sitting in a semicircle on the grass. "Tell us about the farm," they coaxed.

She told them about Trotter and Old Pony and the other pets and animals. She sang little songs she had made up, about the roses and apple blossoms. She taught them to imitate the birds they heard chirping in the trees. Unknown to her and her appreciative audience, Elizabeth was beginning her career as an entertainer!

As the busy days, weeks, and months went by, so did the years. As Elizabeth progressed in school, her head was filled with questions: Why do ships float? What does the sky look like? What are clouds? What are the stars made of? What is a comet? Patient teachers tried to answer her questions.

The course of study was similar to that of the public schools, but with reading done manually. Use of the typewriter was begun early. It was a red-letter day when Elizabeth was able to type a letter to her father:

Dear Papa: Today I am nine years old. I thank you for the present you sent me. This is the first letter I have written on the typewriter, but next year I will learn to write Braille, too, with a stylus and slate.

My music teacher says I have a good ear for music. Do you think she is right? Love to Mama and Ida and Poe and Anne. And love to little Pat and the baby, and to you, dear Papa. Write to me often.

Elizabeth's loyalties were divided now; the end of each school year found her eager to go home, to confide in Madrecita and Ida, to explore again the well-remembered childhood haunts, and to enjoy the younger children. Two new members had been added to the family, a precocious little boy named Pat, and just a year younger, another dark-eyed baby girl, Pauline.

"You sisters are growing up, just as you are, Elizabeth," Madrecita told her that summer. "Anne grows prettier, Ida more capable and Poe helps me so much with the younger children."

Little Patrick, who had begun to talk as soon as he could walk, struggled briefly with Elizabeth's name, and then disposed of the problem with a substitution of his own. "Gee-Gee" he said, and Gee-Gee she remained to family and friends. He adored this affectionate big sister who sang so charmingly to him. Elizabeth promoted family singing at every opportunity, and the blending of her voice with Madrecita's, Ida's and Anne's entranced the little boy, who did his best to join in. The less gifted Mr. Garrett and Poe provided an appreciative audience.

That summer Elizabeth had brought home a Braille slate and a stylus, the sharp instrument with which she punched the dots into the slate to create letters of the alphabet.

"Just think!" she said. "If I had been born a hundred years ago before Louis Braille was born, I should never have been able to read!"

She told her parents the thrilling story of the blind young Frenchman, who in 1829 had devised the 63 characters formed by a series of raised dots to represent letters of the alphabet, as well as punctuation marks and even musical notations. This remarkable man, in spite of his handicap, was well educated in science and music, and became famous in Paris as an organist and violoncellist. "His story is a source of inspiration to the students at the Austin school," she said.

"But I have heard that some are not able to read Braille, as the fingers must be very sensitive," Mr. Garrett said.

"That is true," Elizabeth said, "and a few years ago another kind of bulky letters was invented by an Englishman, William Moon. It is called Moon type, and can be used for simple reading. But Braille readers can work much faster and with more difficult material."

"Our little songbird has learned many things, Madrecita," Mr. Garrett's voice expressed his pride. "We should be very grateful to the Austin school."

His words brought the school vividly to her mind. It was almost time to return, and suddenly she was eager to go. She would miss her family, the singing and laughter, the dear, familiar places. But how good it would be to get back to the typewriter, the piano and other musical intruments, the group singing, and the wonderful world of Braille.

She had no way of knowing that was the last vacation she would spend on the farm.

Chapter 4

CHAPTER 4

High school and junior college courses were available at the Austin school. Elizabeth was now considered an "unclassified" student; consequently, she could proceed at her own pace.

As she advanced she learned that many opportunities were open to the blind, in spite of their visual handicaps. Manual occupations were most commonly followed, and many saleable articles were produced in the manual arts workshop. Elizabeth liked to crochet, and enjoyed creating handmade rugs, sensing their beauty and usefulness.

Other students became skilled in making a variety of articles, including knitted wear, stuffed toys, aprons, and dish towels, mops, brooms, and mattresses.

Learning, however, was an obsession with Elizabeth. She worked to become proficient in reading and writing Braille, so necessary for higher learning if one wished to study independently. She liked languages and history, but geometry dealt her misery as she struggled with angles, rectangles, squares, circles and oblongs fashioned from wood.

> "Geometry completely frustrates me!" she wrote her father. "I think the only thing I have gained from the course is the meaning of a new word, *congruent*."

Fortunately, mathematics had no important part in her plans. Music continued to be her chief interest. The pipe organ, with its great vibrant tones and double keyboard, thrilled her, and she practiced daily on both piano and organ. The piano proved more practical, however, as an accompaniment for voice training and for use in composing and improvising.

> "Elizabeth is becoming a director as well as a performer," Mr. Piner wrote the Garretts. "She has always promoted group singing, and the result is that eight girls with good voices have formed an Octette, with Elizabeth as their accompanist and director. Their harmony is delightful! By invitation, they are filling engagements in churches and private homes. The school is very proud of them, and of their enterprising director."

While Elizabeth made progress at school, much was happening at home. Ida's letters kept her informed.

"Papa is almost too busy to write these days," she wrote, "so I will tell you about his newest venture. He is raising blooded horses, and I think he truly loves it—you know how he likes good horses! He has formed a partnership with a west Texas rancher named John Nance Garner, who, they say, is well known in politics. Papa says raising horses pays better than farming, since the irrigation project fell through."

Elizabeth remembered her father's disappointment at the failure of that undertaking. Water was vitally important to the Pecos Valley farmers, but during dry years, flow from the river was not sufficient to supply their needs. When a few wells were drilled, which produced an encouraging artesian flow of water, Mr. Garrett joined a group of men who financed the drilling of more wells. The results, however, did not justify continuing the project.

Fervently she hoped that the new enterprise would be a success, and she was pleased when Ida sent clippings from West Texas newspapers describing the fine race horses which were coming from the Garner-Garrett stables. But a series of dramatic events, climaxed by the brutal murder of a father and his young son, brought unexpected changes in the Garrett family's affairs.

The vast territory of New Mexico still had its lawless elements. As the population increased and property became more valuable, cattle rustling and land fraud continued to plague honest landholders. This was especially true in the great area of sprawling Lincoln County, now a hotbed of political intrigue.

A highly respected lawyer, Albert J. Fountain, was made special United States District Attorney, to assist officers in apprehending and prosecuting lawbreakers. Formerly an officer in the Union Army assigned to New Mexico, Colonel Fountain had remained in the territory after his military service ended, and like Pat Garrett, had married a pretty young Spanish-Mexican woman. Like Mrs. Garrett, Mariana Perez Fountain was a woman of refinement; gentle, religious and a devoted wife and mother. The Fountains established their home in Las Cruces.

During the twelve years that Colonel Fountain pursued his duties as prosecutor, he came to be feared and hated by certain men. Mrs. Fountain was greatly disturbed by rumored threats against his life.

One day in the early spring of 1896, he left Las Cruces for Lincoln Town, the county seat, where he would take part in a grand jury investigation. Feeling that a child's presence would insure his safety, Mrs. Fountain insisted that their eight-year-old son, Henry, accompany his father.

One hotel in Lincoln belonged to a friend of the Fountains. "Henry will enjoy the trip with you. He will like staying at the hotel," she said. "You will only be away a few days."

The trip would take three or four days by buckboard. The nights would be spent en route at homes of friends at ranches or settlements along the way. Reluctantly, Colonel Fountain agreed to take the little boy along and was rewarded by the child's pleasure.

Arriving in Lincoln, Colonel Fountain succeeded in obtaining indictments charging cattle theft against certain leaders of the outlaw faction, with the trial set for a later date. He then began the journey homeward with little Henry at his side.

Colonel Fountain never reached Las Cruces, where his family anxiously awaited him. His bloodstained buckboard and certain articles of clothing were located near the mysterious great White Sands. Although the horses were found roaming at large next day, the harness cut, father and son had disappeared and were never seen again.

Colonel Fountain and his family were respected and loved. Indignation grew in the community when elected officials did little to solve the case. Newspapers in neighboring states denounced the situation as disgraceful. "There must be no return to the era of Billy the Kid," one editorial declared.

New Mexico's Governor Thornton felt the personal challenge of these sharp criticisms. Many leading citizens had been working diligently for statehood; but the Governor knew the attitude prevailed in Washington that the territory was not qualified to become a state as long as such lawlessness continued.

Many remembered the work of Sheriff Pat Garrett in ending the reign of terror in Lincoln County almost two decades before. They urged Governor Thornton to enlist his services again. As a result, Pat Garrett was offered an appointment as special investigator in the case.

Elizabeth listened intently as Mr. Piner read the lengthy letter from her father:

"I feel that I cannot refuse the Governor's request," the letter concluded. "Perhaps I can serve my state and the cause of justice again. So I must tell you that we are leaving the farm and moving to Las Cruces.

"There will be advantages for the family there. Farm life is not easy for a woman. In Las Cruces, Madrecita will have friends and neighbors to visit. There will be better facilities for Poe, and a good school, the Loretta Academy, for Ida and Anne. A state college has been established there, an advantage for the boys, who are growing up. I believe you will like Las Cruces, too, Elizabeth.

"I am not giving up all ranching interest. We will have a small place a few miles from town, just east of the Organ Mountains, where I can raise horses. This family can't be without good horses!"

After Mr. Piner left her, Elizabeth sat beneath the pecan tree and thought it all over. The prospect of living in town with friends to share the interest of the Garrett sisters was inviting. They were outgrowing the happy pastimes of the farm. She must write Papa at once! She went inside and found the typewriter.

"I am glad the Governor asked you to work on the Fountain case," she wrote. "Oh, I hope you can solve these terrible murders!

"Please, Papa, do not come for me at the end of this term. Just think! I am in high school now. Let me show you that I am becoming independent. Mr. Piner will see me safely aboard the train, and you can meet me in El Paso, for the shorter train ride to Las Cruces. I *am* growing up, today it occurred to me that I should be past the age for climbing trees!"

Before the term ended, however, the pecan tree became her refuge once more. Tragic news came in another letter, which kind Mr. Piner read to her. Gentle Ida, her other "little mother," was dead, a victim of typhoid fever.

In the solitude of leafy branches, Elizabeth found release in a flood of tears. Going home without her beloved Ida, her faithful guide and protector, to welcome her, seemed unthinkable. The future loomed bleak and uncertain.

She recalled something she had overheard before her first trip to Austin: "Elizabeth will grow up, Madrecita," her father had said, "she must be independent, she will not have us always."

Growing up suddenly became very real. She wasn't at all sure she liked it.

It was a balmy May morning when Mr. Piner drove Elizabeth

to the railway station in the two-seated carriage that belonged to the Austin school. The air was fresh and cool after a rain the night before. Roses thrived in the mild climate of mid-southern Texas, and their fragrance was wafted pleasantly on a gentle breeze. Elizabeth breathed deeply, determined to shake off the nervousness she felt.

"I'm sorry I can't stay until your train leaves," Mr. Piner was saying, "but as you know, several parents arrive today to take their children home for the summer, so I must get back to the school."

"Of course, I understand," she smiled as he helped her down from the carriage. She must hide her misgivings from him, he had assured her father that she could make the trip alone. "It was very kind of you to come with me at such a busy time."

"At least I had time for this short visit with one of my favorite students," he said. "Now Mrs. Smith of the Traveler's Aid will see you safely aboard and arrange with the conductor to look after you. And of course your father will meet you in El Paso."

Elizabeth's hand rested lightly on her companion's arm as they entered the busy station. A deluge of noise assailed her ears; shrill voices, hurrying footsteps, and other confusing, unidentifiable sounds.

"Here we are," Mr. Piner said, "and here is Mrs. Smith, Elizabeth." They had stopped at the desk of a plump, silver haired woman who rose and took Elizabeth's hand. "I am glad to see you again, dear. I met you last year, you may remember, when you were traveling with your father."

The girl's expressive face lighted up. "Oh yes, I do remember! I couldn't forget *your* pleasant voice, Mrs. Smith!"

"Thank you! That is indeed a compliment! You have grown, Elizabeth. And Mr. Piner tells me you are making this trip alone."

"We have a very independent girl here," Mr. Piner said with pride, "and one of our best students, too, especially in music. This year she has become our choral director."

"Why, that is marvelous!" Mrs. Smith exclaimed. "It must be very gratifying to accomplish so much."

"Well, it's such fun, it doesn't seem like work. I can never get my fill of music!" The girl's dark eyes sparkled with enthusiasm.

"I must leave you ladies now." Mr. Piner took Elizabeth's hand. "Give my regards to your father, my dear. We will see you in September."

"*Hasta la vista!*" she answered smiling, "until September."

"We will find a good seat for you," Mrs. Smith said. "Let's

see; this should be about right, near the front of the car, just two rows from the washroom. Beyond that is a vestibule, and the dining car. Do you prefer a seat by the window or on the aisle?"

"On the aisle, please." Elizabeth thought of the times when her father had sat by the window, describing the passing scenes.

"Of course, dear. And here is the porter with your suitcase."

"Good morning, Miss Elizabeth," a mellow southern voice said. "You're up early today. I'll just put your suitcase on the rack above your seat."

"It's Sam!" Elizabeth exclaimed in delight.

"Yes, Ma'am!" the cheerful voice replied. "My, how you've grown since last year when you and your daddy made this trip."

"I must go now," Mrs. Smith said. "I know Sam will look after you. And I will ask Mr. Benson, the conductor, to find a congenial seatmate for you if he can. Good luck, dear, we'll see you again in the fall."

Elizabeth sat listening as the sound of their voices receded. Other voices came near, as passengers found their seats in the car. For a moment she felt terribly alone. Her hands moved over the seat cushions. The stiff plush covering felt just the same and had the same musty smell she remembered vividly from her first trip by train to Austin—how many years ago? Seven, eight? How frightened she had been that day even with her father by her side!

But she had been a mere baby then, not quite six years old. So much had happened since, and now she was old enough to travel alone! Of course she wasn't really alone, with Sam and Mr. Benson to help her. Suddenly she felt delightfully grown-up. What fun it would be to tell Ida and Poe and Anne about this experience.

Ida! Her spirits plummeted, and a lump came in her throat. Sometimes she forgot that Ida would not be there. It seemed unreal that Ida was dead; it was like a horrible nightmare.

"Is this seat taken?" a pleasant feminine voice interrupted her thoughts.

"No, I am traveling alone," she answered quickly, "please sit here."

"Thank you. I am Elizabeth Roe, and my destination is El Paso."

"I am going to El Paso too. And *my* name is Elizabeth, Elizabeth Garrett."

"Well, we two Elizabeths should get along quite well! But I am selfish to take the window seat. Wouldn't you prefer it?"

Elizabeth felt a glow of pleasure. So she appeared like any other girl to this new acquaintance! She hastened to set her right.

"The aisle seat is more convenient for me," she said simply. "You see, I am blind. I usually travel with my father, and he sits by the window so he can see for me."

"Then perhaps you will allow me that pleasure. I should begin by describing *myself*. First, I am *Miss* Roe, a spinster school teacher; medium height and weight, medium brown hair, blue eyes, just a very medium person you might say!" She laughed. "Even my age, which is about twice yours, I imagine. Oh, here is the conductor."

"Good morning, ladies," Mr. Benson spoke, "I will take your tickets now. I see you have both found good company." He punched their tickets and clipped two receipt stubs above the window. "Be sure to ring for me or Sam, if you should need anything."

"Thank you, I am sure we shall get along very well," Miss Roe replied.

Elizabeth breathed a sigh of relief. How much simpler to be aided by this gracious lady than to have to ask Sam or Mr. Benson to escort her to the dining car or the unfamiliar lavoratory door! She had expected to sleep through the night in her Pullman seat, but with her new friend's guidance, she could make use of the lower berth Mr. Piner reserved for her.

"Now tell me more about *you*," Miss Roe said, as the train moved away from the noisy station. "I only know what I can *see*, a well-mannered girl with lovely brown eyes, shining dark braids, smooth olive skin . . . the only medium thing about *you*, I think, is your size—about average for a young girl of fifteen or sixteen."

"Only fourteen," Elizabeth blushed.

"You look older. Have you made this trip often?"

"Yes, with my father. I have attended the Austin School for the Blind since I was small. Each fall, we took the train from El Paso to Austin, and in the spring he came back for me. This year, I asked to make the trip alone."

"Then your family lives in El Paso?"

"No, but quite near there, in Las Cruces. They moved there from our ranch home in the Pecos Valley."

"Oh, I know Las Cruces! A delightful place. It has lovely gardens and orchards, with irrigation from the Rio Grande."

"Madrecita—that's my mother—she likes it there very much."

"Madrecita! What a charming name!"

"It means 'little mother' in Spanish. My mother *is* Spanish, or rather Spanish and Aztec, and she *is* small. Last summer we found that I was taller than she!" She smiled, thinking of the day when Anne had taken all the family measurements. Little Pat was growing so fast, he showed signs of becoming another *Juan Largo*, or "Long John," as the native ranch hands affectionately called Mr. Garrett. "But my father is very tall," Elizabeth went on, "six feet four, in fact."

"Your father must be Pat Garrett!" Miss Roe exclaimed. "My pupils have studied about him in our new history books; about his work in ending the Lincoln County War in New Mexico! I read recently in the El Paso paper that he has been elected sheriff again."

"Elizabeth nodded. "First he was appointed special investigator in the Fountain murder case, then elected sheriff."

"The Fountain case! I have read of that too, of course. Colonel Fountain lived in El Paso at one time and was highly thought of. People there have followed the case closely. And last month I read that your father had secured indictments against three men believed to be guilty of the murders, the same men who had been originally indicted by Colonel Fountain for cattle theft."

"The case was dropped after his death," Elizabeth said, "just as the murderers knew it would be. Now they are being tried again, but not in Lincoln or Las Cruces. Their lawyers said they could not get a fair trial in either place so the judge set the trial in Hillsboro, another county seat. My father wrote that the trial should be over by the time I get home."

"Let us hope the guilty will be punished," Miss Roe said earnestly. "It was indeed a terrible crime."

"Madrecita worries," Elizabeth confided. "An officer of the law makes enemies. But she knows that my father is again doing the work he likes best."

"We have so much to talk about," Miss Roe said ruefully, "I can see this trip will be all too short! It's too bad, but we do have to take time out to sleep!"

Elizabeth laughed. The trip she had faced with trepidation was turning out to be a happy experience. They had lunch in the dining car, and later, dinner with much conversation in between. Then came the new experience of preparing for bed in the ladies' lounge car, and climbing into the Pullman berth, where Elizabeth was soon lulled to sleep by the subdued clickety-click of the rails as the train rushed through the night across the wide Texas plains.

They had scarcely finished breakfast next morning when they heard the conductor's resonant call: "El Paso next stop! Thirty minutes to El Paso!"

The train ground to a stop with a great hissing of steam and ringing of bells. "Take my arm, dear," Miss Roe said, as they rose to make their way to the end of the coach. "Sam will bring your bag."

Elizabeth's heart was beating fast. Papa would be waiting! He would be glad to know she had made the trip with no difficulty. She was eager to have him meet her new friend.

"Elizabeth! Gee-Gee!" she heard a familiar feminine voice shrieking. "Here we are! Here!" She was immediately half smothered in Anne's enthusiastic embrace.

"Anne! Where is Papa?"

"Papa couldn't come, he's still in Hillsboro. But Bettie came in his place—oh, this is Bettie Quesenberry, one of my schoolmates at Loretto Academy."

"How nice of you to come, Bettie," Elizabeth said. "You must both meet Miss Roe. She was so kind and helpful on the train."

"It is a real pleasure to meet you, girls," Miss Roe said cordially. "Elizabeth and I have had a very pleasant trip. We find we have much in common."

"How *nice!*" Anne exclaimed, with her typical enthusiasm. "Papa always says we don't have to worry about Gee-Gee. She has the knack for attracting the most interesting friends."

"Gee-Gee?" Miss Roe smiled.

"Just a pet name for Elizabeth," Anne explained, "our little brother Pat gave her that name when he was learning to talk. Now she can't get rid of it."

"Will you have lunch with us here, Miss Roe?" Bettie asked. "We can continue our visit, as we have a two-hour wait for our train to Las Cruces."

"No, thank you, I must say goodbye now. I see my friends waiting with their carriage."

"Thank you again, Miss Roe," Elizabeth said. "*Hasta la vista!*" Miss Roe took her hand. "Yes, my dear, until we meet again! And I am sure we shall!"

"What a lovely lady!" Anne took her sister's arm and the three girls entered the station. They made their way to the lunch room where big fans droned pleasantly overhead, providing a welcome relief from the hot southwestern sun.

"Wasn't it just *wonderful* that Bettie and I could come to meet you?" Anne bubbled, when they were seated. "Papa was worried at first, he wouldn't think of allowing me to come alone! And of course Mama couldn't leave the new baby. But Bettie came to the rescue!"

"Well, I have made the trip before, to visit our friends, the

Pattersons. And Mr. Garrett said since I am older—" Bettie made a wry face—"practically an old maid, now that I am sixteen—"

"Papa and Bettie's father have become very good friends," Anne broke in, "and they agreed that we could come on the train yesterday, spending the night with the Pattersons. Then today, Judge Patterson was in court and Mrs. Patterson had a Woman's Club meeting, so we came *alone* on the street car from their house to the depot! It was such fun!"

Elizabeth relaxed with a sigh of pure pleasure. The tension of the trip, and the wrench she always felt in leaving the security of the school and familiar surroundings subsided. It was a joy to be with vivacious Anne and her attractive friend. Instinctively, she responded to qualities in Bettie's voice which denoted dependability and calm. How important voices were to the blind! The surest clue to identity and personality, the speaking voice!

"I love the scent of mint," Elizabeth sniffed appreciatively as she stirred her iced tea, "and the chicken sandwich smells delicious, too!"

"I never *knew* anyone who could get so much pleasure out of smells!" Anne exclaimed.

"Well, it isn't always pleasure," Elizabeth countered, "some of the smells are far from pleasant, I can tell you! But my nose is a great guide."

"I can tell you, Bettie, it is downright uncanny, the way this sister of mine manages," Anne's lilting voice held a note of pride. "With her sensitive touch and her keen ears, as well as that remarkable nose—you can be sure she doesn't miss much! More than once, I have had the feeling that Gee-Gee sees more than I do!"

Elizabeth's expressive face grew serious. "I am really very lucky. There are children at the school who don't hear well; they are terribly handicapped. And some are not as alert as others. And think of this—there are some unfortunate children who were born entirely deaf, as well as blind! They are not accepted at the Austin school."

"Are they not able to enter school at *all?*" Bettie asked, appalled at the thought of these children, condemned to a life of silence and darkness.

"There is a school in Massachusetts, established only a few years ago, where they are being taught to read," Elizabeth said. "It must be very difficult for them. If I couldn't hear, I would truly feel handicapped. From all the wonderful descriptions I hear, I have a definite picture of how things look, even colors! Of course, I will never know whether I am right." A wistful expression flitted over her mobile features. She shrugged. "Enough of such serious talk! Tell me about the children and Madrecita. How is Poe?"

"Poe isn't strong, but he gets about quite well," Anne said, "and he has a new interest. He helps Mama with the cooking!"

It had always been Ida, assuming happily but seriously her responsibility as oldest child, who had been her mother's dependable helper. The black grief threatened Elizabeth again, as she thought of the many hours Ida had spent looking after the younger children, when her mother was occupied with the housework, cooking or sewing; or patiently acting as guide and teacher to the demanding little girl Elizabeth had been!

Resolutely, she shook off her sorrowful memories and came back to the present.

"Mama can use some help, I'm sure," she said, "with Papa, and let's see—how many children to cook for? There's you, Anne, and Poe and Pat, and now baby Pauline. And I make one more, when I'm home. A family of seven!"

"Well, Pauline doesn't eat much yet!" Anne giggled.

"But I'm there half the time to eat my share," Bettie said, "so that makes eight! Poe *is* a good cook, he is becoming really expert at Mexican dishes. Wait till you taste his *tortillas*! And his *enchiladas*! We call him *El Chef*!"

Suddenly Elizabeth could hardly wait to get home. As if he had read her mind, a conductor came through the waiting room to the lunch room door. "All aboard for Las Cruces! All aboard!"

"I'll pay our check," Bettie said efficiently. "You girls go ahead, and I'll show the porter where our bags are."

"Here are two seats, facing each other, just right for us!" Anne said. "Isn't it just marvelous the way everything happens?"

"There are so many things to talk about," Elizabeth said, "I have hundreds of questions to ask!"

"Start any time," Bettie laughed, "the walking encyclopedia, that's me!"

The train began to move, with the noisy screeching and grinding that always hurt Elizabeth's ears, then more smoothly as they got under way.

"Now we're leaving the railway yards," Anne said, settling back to enjoy the ride. "There are several tracks here, Gee-Gee, and a lot of freight cars on a side track, waiting to be unloaded, I suppose. Those clanging bell-like gongs are the signals at street crossings."

Elizabeth listened, alert and eager, smiling to herself at Anne's unconscious imitation of their father's way of helping her to see the world about her. How dear they all were, her wonderful family!

"When will Papa be home?" she asked.

"He could be there now; the trial may have ended yesterday," Anne said.

"My father says that all the Las Cruces citizens are so relieved that those men have been brought to trial at last," Bettie said. "Just think, three years have passed since Colonel Fountain and his little son were murdered so cruelly."

"And their bodies were never found!" Anne said. "Papa says that has made the case much harder to solve. Most people believe they are buried somewhere in the White Sands; they know the murder happened near the Sands, where the buckboard and bloody clothing were found. But there are so many miles of those lonely sand dunes."

"Little Henry Fountain was only eight years old," Elizabeth said. The horror of the cowardly deed swept over her anew, as she thought of her small brothers, so dear to her. "If those men are guilty, they *should* be punished."

"Papa is very sure they are guilty," Anne said.

"And my father says the governor is anxious to have the case cleared up," Bettie added. "He says New Mexico can never become a state until we change our reputation as a wild and lawless territory."

Suddenly they realized the train was slowing down. "Why, we're almost there!" Anne exclaimed. "How fast the train went!"

"Las Cruces! Las Cruces!" the conductor called, and they hurried to gather up their coats and handbags. Bettie peered out the window. "Oh, I see my father waiting."

"But Papa isn't with him!" Anne said.

Elizabeth felt a pang of disappointment. That meant her father was not back from Hillsboro. But he would be home soon, and there would be much to talk about. Meantime, she would have a joyous reunion with Madrecita and the children.

Sheriff Garrett returned from Hillsboro a bitterly disappointed man. The trial had ended and the three suspects in the murder case were acquitted! The grueling work he had carried out for months had come to nothing.

He resolved, however, to hide his deep discouragement from his family and was able to forget his problems temporarily in the joy of having Elizabeth home. Poe put forth his best efforts, too, in assisting Madrecita with a festive meal that included favorite dishes of the returned travelers.

Chapter 5

CHAPTER 5

One morning Mr. Quesenberry announced that he had a full day's business in town. Would Bettie or her mother like to drive in with him? Mrs. Quesenberry declined; she had sewing to do, but Bettie accepted readily. It would be a good time to visit the Garrett girls.

The entire Garrett family intrigued her. She had gone with her mother to make a neighborly call on Mrs. Garrett some weeks before. They had found her enchanting, a petite, dark-eyed lady with a soft voice so well suited to her native language. Although her command of English was limited, she endeavored politely to carry on a conversation with her visitors, who spoke no Spanish. At times she called on Anne or Poe for help, when a phrase was beyond her. Bettie marveled at the ease with which the children spoke either language.

She had often seen Sheriff Garrett riding through the streets on one of his fine horses. He was a striking figure in his typical western attire, from his handmade boots to his wide Stetson hat, always wearing his famous six-guns in their handsome handtooled leather holsters.

Now Bettie was eager to know Elizabeth better. "I would like to take the Garrett girls for a drive in the country today while you are busy," she said. "Elizabeth seemed eager to know more about our valley."

Her father noded approval. "She is the blind daughter, isn't she?"

"Yes, but it's an interesting thing. She has lovely eyes, they show no sign of her affliction, as far as appearance goes. One almost forgets she can't see, she is so—so *aware*, she can really see so much with her other senses. It's fantastic!"

"Her father tells me she is showing considerable musical talent," Mr. Quesenberry said. It's a fine thing for a blind person to have that talent. So many careers are closed to them."

"Why not bring your friends out here for lunch today," Bettie's mother interposed. "I would like to know this girl, too!"

They got an early start, and the air was still cool and fresh when they drew up before the courthouse on the public square. As was the custom in all early New Mexican villages, the town square, or plaza, was dominated by the Catholic church. Built of *adobe*, the church had thick plastered walls and small stained glass windows, protecting the interior from the heat of summer and the cold of winter. The builders had followed a Spanish mission type of architecture, and heavy handcarved wooden doors had been artfully fitted into arched entrances. Above the main entrance, a sturdy bell tower, topped by a simple wooden cross, held a treasured church bell which the first Franciscan Fathers had brought from Spain.

Lilac bushes abounded in the plaza, planted and tended by the Catholic Sisters. They were watered by little ditches that branched out from the main *acequia*, and were now in full bloom, their lovely purple clusters of blossoms spreading a delicious fragrance in the air.

"Come back for me about five; I'll meet you here," Mr. Quesenberry handed Bettie the reins. "I have business at the bank and some meetings to attend, so I'll be busy all day. Be sure Ginger has water around noon."

"Of course, Daddy!" Bettie was slightly indignant. As if she would neglect Ginger! "See you at five, then. Is Mr. Garrett at home now?"

"He should be. He is meeting with a group of citizens this afternoon. We want to persuade him to run for re-election this fall, but it may not be easy, after what happened at Hillsboro."

Bettie drove down the narrow, dusty street leading away from the business section. The patios and gardens of the low, brown houses were half-hidden by adobe walls, but many blossoming fruit trees could be seen, and climbing roses, in all their riotous colors, spilled over the walls.

Suddenly she was keenly aware of the beauty around her. How could she convey these impressions to one who could not see?

At the Garretts' front gate, she stepped down from the buggy and looped Ginger's halter rein through the iron ring in the hitching post. Suddenly the screen door flew open and Anne rushed out.

"I saw you coming! We *hoped* you would be here today! Papa said your father was coming in town for a meeting—" she turned as Mr. Garrett appeared. "Papa! Bettie came!"

"So I see!" His eyes were twinkling as he joined them. "It's a pleasure to see you again, Bettie. It was good of you to meet Elizabeth in El Paso. I have been hearing a great deal about that trip."

"I enjoyed it very much. It was my first opportunity to meet Elizabeth. We had so much to talk about!"

Mr. Garrett smiled. "Yes, from what she has told me, I gather you girls are *muy simpatico*! I hope you will visit us often."

"Oh, I shall! And the girls must visit me, too. I love our farm, I want to show them some of my favorite places."

"Elizabeth would enjoy that, I'm sure. She grew up on a farm and took to it like a duck to water. Well, I must get down to the courthouse. *Hasta la vista*, ladies!"

"Bettie!" Elizabeth called from the doorway, "Please come in!" The girls embraced, and they went into the sunny living room, where Poe was helping little Pat with a set of building blocks. Mrs. Garrett came in from the bedroom, where she had just put baby Pauline down for her morning nap. "It is nice to see you again, Bettie," she said in her halting English. "Elizabeth has talked much of you. Please be at home, *mi casa es su casa, comprende?* My house is yours!"

"Yes, thank you, I *do* understand. But today, if you are willing, I should like to take the girls for a long drive in the valley. They should see the orchards, they're so lovely now—" she paused in embarrassment, realizing that Elizabeth would not be able to see the beauty of the verdant fields and blossoming orchards.

"Oh, I would love that!" Elizabeth spoke quickly. "Anne and I have walked all over town; she has described the gardens and trees and lilacs—but the country! It must be like the farm where we lived. It would give me the greatest pleasure to see it with your eyes."

Bettie blinked away unexpected tears. "It's a deal!" she said gaily. "We'll have a grand tour. With Anne's help, I'll give you a detailed description."

"I can't go!" Anne said dolefully. "I promised Sister Angela that I would help with the book stacks at the school library! She wants them in good order, now that the school term is over."

"Elizabeth will have to depend on my limited ability, then," Bettie said cheerfully. "There will be other times for the three of us. First, we will drive across the river to my home. Mother wants us to have lunch with her. After lunch we will drive down the lower road to Mesilla and see our fine new State College building, then back up the main road to town. It's kind of a circle drive, but we should make it easily by five o'clock in time to meet my father."

As they trotted toward the river bridge Bettie was silent. How did one describe things to a blind person? Elizabeth had never seen anything so there was no base for comparison. Bettie's good sense took a hand, and she approached the subject without embarrassment.

"Well," she said, "we started out to show you the scenery. Now, tell me how best to go about it."

Elizabeth was delighted with her friend's frank, open manner. She shrank from being an object of pity or special consideration. "Just tell me what you see," she said, "and I'll probably interrupt you with hundreds of questions. Oh, we're crossing the bridge! Tell me about the river."

Bettie glanced at her in surprise, then realized that the vibration of the wheels on the wide, rough planks and the rumbling sound so different from that made by the wheels on the dirt road had given Elizabeth the clue.

"Well, it doesn't look much like the silvery Rio Grande poets have written about," Bettie said, "although it might look like that by moonlight. Normally, it doesn't have much water in it, and you would see just a wide, sandy river bed with a narrow stream flowing through, but just now, it is flowing at full tide after the spring thaws in the mountains north of us. So now it is wide and swift and the water is reddish brown from the soil washed down from many streams and *arroyos* that drain into it." She glanced at the other girl. What did reddish brown mean to someone who had never seen the soil? She was reassured by the rapt look on Elizabeth's face.

"The farmers are taking advantage of the spring flow," she continued. "They're all busy diverting the water from the main *acequia*, which begins a good many miles north of here, where the terrain allows the water to flow from the river into the big main ditch. Oh dear! This must sound terribly confusing."

"Not at all!" Elizabeth assured her. "I know about irrigation ditches. When we lived on the farm—Papa always called it a ranch, he raised cattle and horses as well as crops—we had irrigation water from another river. The main *acequia* was very close to our house, and it was a source of worry to our mother."

"With small children playing about, I should think so!" Bettie agreed.

"We were taught that we must never play near the big ditch of course, and there were fences which protected the smaller children. But we had to learn to cross it, as it ran between our yard and the barn and orchard, where we spent much of our time. There was a narrow footbridge, rather high above the water. My father showed me how to cross it alone."

Bettie was incredulous. "You crossed alone? I get dizzy, even now at my age, crossing a footbridge."

"Maybe at times there is an advantage in not being able to *see* danger," Elizabeth said. "My father insisted that I be allowed to roam about the place freely. I can hear him now: 'She must learn caution, Madrecita, but caution without fear.' He spent many hours teaching me the things I needed to know; how to climb a tree or a ladder and get down again, just where the stairs to the hayloft were located, and how to cross alone over that bridge."

"Your father must be a very unusual man," Bettie said.

"He was very patient! I learned how the fields were watered

because he let me help him when he opened the gates to let the water through. They were made of wood and were more like doors, really, holding the water in check." She laughed. "A lot of help I must have been! He helped me to understand just how the system worked, though, by allowing me to use my hands, to help lift the sturdy wooden gates and to feel the force of the water as it rushed out to flood the fields."

When they reached the large house, Bettie helped Elizabeth down from the buggy and led her in to meet Mrs. Quesenberry.

"We will have our lunch here on the screened porch," Mrs. Quesenberry said. "It's such a lovely day."

"I smell apple blossoms!" Elizabeth sniffed with obvious pleasure.

"Yes, the orchard is very near, and the breeze is cooperating nicely this morning! Now I have cold ham and hot rolls and milk, but shouldn't we enjoy some of our strawberries today? I noticed this morning they are ready for eating. Would you pick a bowlful, Bettie?"

"Let me help!" Elizabeth exclaimed. As the girls stooped over the low green plants laden with inviting red fruit, Bettie watched in amazement as her friend's sensitive fingers deftly found the berries which were just right for eating.

"They smell so delicious!" Elizabeth sniffed ecstatically. "I'm so glad I have a nose!"

Bettie's laughter rang out merrily. "Well, I had never thought of being glad I have a nose, but it would be sad to be without one, wouldn't it?"

"Especially in spring and summer, with all the lovely smells floating about," Elizabeth said. They washed the ripe red fruit under the pump outside the kitchen door, and joined Mrs. Quesenberry at the small table set on the wide, cool porch.

"Here is a pitcher of cream for the strawberries," Mrs. Quesenberry said. "I hope you girls have good appetites."

She needn't have worried. Elizabeth was sure she had never had a more delicious meal.

Afterward they drove down a country lane to the village of Mesilla and across the river again. Here they turned north on the main road leading back to Las Cruces.

"The campus of our new college is to our right," Bettie said. "I can see the main building. It's a two-story red brick, as impressive as the school's name, New Mexico College of Agricultural and Mechanical Arts! I hope I can enroll there after I graduate from the Academy, although Mama says it seems more suitable for boys. She thinks it will be fine for my young brother, Joe, later on."

"My parents plan to enroll my brothers there, too, when they're older," Elizabeth said. "How lucky they are."

"Now I must tell you about the mountains to the east of us," Bettie said. "They are very close to us, really, only a few miles away. They have deep canyons and bare granite peaks, which rise straight up abruptly, and look something like the pipes of an organ."

"The Organ Mountains!" Elizabeth exclaimed. "I think I know how they look! When I began the study of the organ, my instructor showed me in detail how the instrument is constructed, he even had me climb a ladder so that I could run my hands over the pipes."

Bettie closed her eyes, trying to imagine the exploration of a world without sight. Ginger trotted steadily along, needing no guidance on the familiar road. When Bettie opened her eyes, she looked about her with a new awareness, as if she were seeing this lovely valley for the first time. The road wound along under huge old cottonwood trees, and the light summer breeze brought the faint scent of freshly cut alfalfa and blossoming orchards from the fields across the river. On the right, the mesa, dotted with low growth of sage and chamisa, rose gradually toward the canyon-creased mountains. Here and there, stands of stately blossoming yucca appeared.

"Let's take a side road here," Bettie said, "and stop for a moment. You must see the yucca while it's in full bloom." They got out of the buggy, and Elizabeth's seeing hands began their examination of the stately desert plant. One single tall stalk bearing the great cluster of creamy, waxen blossoms grew from each clump of sturdy green spike-tipped leaves.

She was silent as they resumed their drive. Her mind was busy, storing up the impressions of this day. What a splendid guide and teacher her new friend had turned out to be!

"We have company!" Bettie exclaimed suddenly. "A funny bird, a roadrunner, is showing off, running up the road straight ahead of us!"

"Oh, I know who he is, the chapparal bird. Papa tells me he can out-run a fast horse!"

"He *is* fast, all right, and quite a character, too. They say he belongs to the cuckoo family, but he looks like a long-tailed skinny turkey! He's a true native of the Southwest."

"Little Paisano! My fellow countryman!" Elizabeth murmured. "A native, like me."

The Garrett and Quesenberry families met frequently that summer at acequia parties. The big canals had once given Madrecita such a fright but now provided excellent swimming for the adventurous. There were late evening picnics, too, with an abundance of fried chicken, sandwiches and lemonade, and always talk of the Organ Mountains: their height—their ruggedness—their changing appearance and color in the sunset glow—their rocky towering pinnacles which resembled the massive pipes of a huge organ carved from solid rock. Elizabeth listened, storing the descriptions in her mind.

The families met again at the Fourth of July celebration. It ended with a dance at the skating rink, the only available place for public dancing. The music of guitars and violins put the crowd in a festive mood. There was fun for everyone, fathers, mothers, and children, but especially for the young people.

"You look pretty, Gee-Gee," little Patrick said, "but sort of grown-up, too." Elizabeth was lovely in an ankle-length ruffled dress with a blue sash. Her long black hair hung in a single braid tied with a blue ribbon.

"She does look grown-up tonight," Mr. Garrett agreed. "Perhaps my grown-up daughter will honor me with a dance?"

She could think of no greater pleasure than waltzing with her adored father. He was a splendid dancer, and had taught her the waltz, the schottische, and the polka. She couldn't know, as others did, that they made a striking couple, the tall, distinguished sheriff and his graceful daughter. After a time, they found themselves alone on the floor as the other dancers stopped to watch them. The evening became another of Elizabeth's cherished memories.*

*A few years later, some of the impressions of that happy summer were incorporated into three of her many notable songs of the southwest: *O Fair New Mexico*, *The Yucca*, and *Paisano*. The first became New Mexico's official state song; the popular appeal of the others influenced the choice of the state flower, the yucca; and the state bird, the chapparal.

Chapter 6

CHAPTER 6

Back at school, Elizabeth became more and more engrossed in music. She spent many hours at the piano, practicing and working with Braille notes and instructions; then, for relaxation, composing and transcribing into Braille the verses that filled her head, clamoring for expression.

She kept up a lively correspondence with Bettie and Anne.

"Now that I am using the typewriter, I shall bombard you with letters," she wrote. "It will give me the practice I need!"

When their letters came in reply, she always waited for Mr. Piner to read them to her. "Letters should not be public property," she told him, "but you are like my own family."

It was Bettie who first wrote that Mr. Garrett had been defeated in his campaign for re-election as sheriff.

"My father says those men who were on trial have a lot of influence in politics now. They are afraid of Mr. Garrett. They know they can't control him, and they worked hard to defeat him."

"Papa is discouraged," Anne wrote. "Oh, Gee-Gee, you couldn't believe the things that happened during the campaign. Ugly rumors were spread about our dear Papa, and even about poor Colonel Fountain, although he has been dead all this time! They said 'white' citizens don't want public officials with half-breed families! And they tried to make a hero of Billy the Kid, who was a murderer and outlaw twenty years ago!

"They said Papa shot his *friend* in cold blood! His friend! Poor Papa, he doesn't know I heard these stories, and I think he has kept them from Madrecita. He assures us everything will be all right, he can raise horse again. A good thing he still has the land east of the mountains."

Elizabeth felt a growing anxiety for her father. His political opponents were dangerous and powerful. The cruel murderers of Colonel Fountain were still at large, and they hated Pat Garrett, who had tried to bring them to justice. The dream of honest men for the rule of law and order in New Mexico was still unfulfilled.

The century was drawing to a close. The year 1900 was ushered in with momentous happenings over the nation. Newspapers carried glowing stories of the opportunities and advances predicted for the new century. Fate decreed that some of these events would affect the Garrett family.

Theodore Roosevelt, hero of the Spanish-American War, who had led his famous Rough Riders to victory at San Juan Hill, was now Vice President of the United States. The Garrett family felt a very personal interest in TR, as he was affectionately known, for he was a close friend of Mr. Garrett's former ranching partner in West Texas, John Nance Garner, who was now serving in the United States Congress.

On September 14, 1901, shocking news was flashed over the nation by telegraph. President McKinley had been assassinated! On that day, Theodore Roosevelt became President of the United States.

Shortly after, through the influence of Congressman Garner, Pat Garrett was appointed to a high political post, Collector of Customs, at the El Paso Port of Entry between Mexico and the United States.

"Papa says two old friends appeared before the President, in his behalf, when the appointment was under consideration," Anne wrote. "They were Congressman Garner of Texas and General Lew Wallace. You know, of course, that General Wallace was governor when Papa was assigned to arrest Billy the Kid."

Elizabeth was pleased and happy at the recognition her father was receiving. General Wallace had become a highly respected author. Although he now lived in the east, much of his noted book, *Ben Hur*, had been written while he lived in New Mexico. He had a genuine affection for the Southwest and its people.

Collector of Customs was a position of importance in the Southwest, usually given to a leading citizen of adjoining New Mexico Territory. The office had once been held by Colonel Albert Fountain.

What changes took place now in the Garretts' way of living! They left their modest adobe house in Las Cruces, with its scrubbed pine floors and white plastered walls, and moved into a fine brick house in El Paso, where they were neighbors of Judge and Mrs. Patterson, friends of the Quesenberry family.

Madrecita had comforts and luxuries she had never dreamed of! There were carpeted floors and a sweeper to clean them;

papered walls instead of plastered adobe, and modern plumbing. There were great blocks of ice delivered to the box on the back porch, green vegetables delivered to her door by vendors, the heavy wash sent to the laundry, and the final luxury, a part-time helper to assist with the housework!

Elizabeth now made the trip alone from Austin to El Paso with ease. Summer vacations in their new home were joyous times for Elizabeth and Anne. Old Mexico lay only a stone's throw away, across the International Bridge that spanned the Rio Grande, the boundary between the two countries. The sisters rode on the streetcar to the bridge, then walked across to visit the colorful shops in Juarez, thrilled by the knowledge that they were in a foreign country! They shopped for dainty handmade dresses and exotic perfumes, conversing easily with the shopkeepers in fluent Spanish, finding renewed pleasure in their Spanish heritage. And all the while, Anne's vivid descriptions were stored in Elizabeth's retentive mind.

There was no lack of entertainment. They went to magic lantern shows, where Anne described the projected scenes to Elizabeth *soto voce*, when the narrator failed to be explicit enough. There were Sunday evening band concerts in San Jacinto Park, El Paso's main "plaza;" and often the thrilling entertainment of a traveling summer chautauqua, bringing dramatic readings, plays, and music to the city. El Paso was becoming the cultural center of the Southwest.

They rode about the neighborhood on a shiny new bicycle built for two which their father insisted they should have, although Mrs. Garrett thought it rather bold. "They go so fast!" she said anxiously. "Isn't it dangerous?"

Mr. Garrett only laughed at her. "They can take care of themselves, Madrecita. We must keep up with the times. We're living in a new era, who knows what the twentieth century will bring? Why, you and I may soon be riding in one of those new horseless carriages!"

"Oh, no!" she protested. "They go even faster than the bicycles, as fast as twenty miles an hour, I have heard!"

"Even faster, maybe thirty! But don't worry, *querida*. We'll be safe enough, when the time comes. *Ten fe**, remember. That is what you have always said to us."

Have faith! Yes, she had always had faith, in her husband, and in a divine power that protected her family. She resolved to be less fearful and to try harder to enjoy the many pleasures good

---

*Ten fe — familiar form for *tenga fe*.

68

fortune had bestowed upon them.

The Pattersons bought a new Edison Graphophone, and invited their neighbors to see it. "We have two records of Caruso's singing, and one of Sousa's band," Mrs. Patterson told the girls. "But before you hear them, Elizabeth, you must see how the machine and the records are made."

She guided Elizabeth's hands first over the small box on which a large horn was mounted, then over the horn from which the sound would emerge, and finally over the black wax cylinders that mysteriously held the magical music. They listened in awe as the magnificent voice of the Italian tenor poured out into the room, and almost in disbelief, to the stirring strains of "The Stars and Stripes Forever," played by Sousa's band.

Elizabeth was sure she was the luckiest of girls. Summer vacations were pure pleasure, and school terms were challenging and exciting.

"I know you are concerned about Elizabeth's future," Mr. Piner wrote Mr. Garrett. "She will graduate in a few months, with high honors. Music continues to be her chief interest, and she shows ability as a director, as well as a composer and performer. The staff of the school and many music lovers in Austin will miss her and the Octette, after they graduate and leave us. Elizabeth has an excellent voice, and by the time she graduates, I believe she will be qualified to teach voice as well as piano."

On a warm, sunny morning in late May the train from Austin pulled into the El Paso station. One of the first passengers to appear was a young woman modishly dressed in a high-collared white shirtwaist and dark skirt that touched the tops of her high buttoned black shoes. Her dark hair was neatly arranged in a coronet of shining braids; the current vogue for a high, ratted pompadour had proved unmanageable for Elizabeth in spite of her best efforts. With the braids she needed no assistance.

She knew her father would be waiting. She hoped fervently for his sake that she looked grown-up; she wanted him to know that his dream for her was realized, that she was now ready to take her place in society and to make a living for herself if necessary.

Mr. Garrett *was* waiting, appropriately dressed for this happy occasion and in keeping with his position in pin-striped trousers, dark coat and hat, and vest ornamented by a heavy gold watch chain. Confident that he was there, Elizabeth waved a white paper in the air. He smiled, recognizing the emblem of victory, her diploma!

She was fairly smothered by the enthusiastic embraces of Mama, Poe, Pat and Anne when they entered the big brick house. "We sent Papa alone to meet you," Anne bubble, "so we could have everything ready!"

"The surprises, for Gee-Gee," Pat said, dancing with excitement. "You are first, Mama!" And Mrs. Garrett gently placed a warm, wriggling little bundle in Elizabeth's arms. "Your new baby brother," she said. "This is little Jarvis, not yet a month old."

"What a lovely surprise!" Elizabeth cradled the little form with one arm, gently tracing his tiny features with the fingers of her free hand.

"Now you know why we were too busy to go to your graduation!" Anne said. "Let me hold him now, you have still more to see!"

"Little Oscar is next," Mrs. Garrett said. "You remember, he was barely walking when you left last fall. He is so big now and talks very well."

Elizabeth gave the baby to Anne, and knelt to put her arms around the toddler. "Oh, he *has* grown, and so has our family! How many now? Poe, Anne, Pat, Pauline, my little Oscar, and the tiny one! Are you sure there is room for me?"

"This is a big house, there is room for all my children," Mrs. Garrett spoke with pride. "Now come into the parlor. Papa has more to show you."

Elizabeth was speechless when her father placed her hands on the keyboard of a fine new piano. "You will need this for your music lessons," he said, "and here is something else you should have." He placed a Swiss watch in her hand. "See, the face has raised numbers, you can tell the time easily."

Tears of happiness filled her eyes, as she threw her arms about him. "Oh, thank you, dear Papa. You know I love surprises, but I never expected such grand gifts as these. Now I am ready to start with my pupils."

"And with that watch, no excuse for being late," Anne said.

"But where are the pupils?" Poe asked.

Elizabeth laughed. "A very good question! But they'll come, you'll see. I may even place a notice in the El Paso Herald-Post."

First, however, the Garretts insisted that Elizabeth and Anne enjoy a vacation. Both girls had worked hard at school. Anne was now enrolled in an El Paso school for girls where she sometimes found the rigid discipline imposed by the Sisters a bit too exacting for her tastes! She welcomed another carefree interval with Elizabeth.

They were overjoyed to renew their acquaintance with Elizabeth Roe, who was also spending her vacation at home. Now the three of them visited Juarez, attended concerts in the park, and shopped for summer clothes. At Miss Roe's invitation, they attended a church nearby, where a splendid new pipe organ had been installed. The organ was Elizabeth's favorite instrument. With her friend's cooperation, she arranged for a regular time for practice at the church.

As guests of Mrs. Patterson, they attended teas and concerts in homes of prominent El Paso residents, and the increasingly popular affairs sponsored by the Woman's Club, an active group of women who largely controlled the cultural events of the city.

One afternoon Mrs. Patterson came calling on the Garretts. Mrs. Garrett welcomed her guest graciously, and Anne and Elizabeth, following the example of their mother, were poised hostesses, serving tall glasses of iced tea and dainty little cakes which they had made that morning.

"Delicious!" Mrs. Patterson said. "You are teaching your daughters to be good cooks, Mrs. Garrett. I really came to ask a favor of Elizabeth."

Elizabeth waited, trying to imagine what she might do for this friend who had been so kind to her family.

"I am entertaining the Woman's Club in my home later in the month," Mrs. Patterson continued, "and I must arrange a program. Will you sing for us?"

"Oh, yes! I would love to sing!" Elizabeth's face was radiant. Then she hesitated. "That is, if I am good enough?"

"Certainly you are, my dear. The ladies are eager to hear you. They have heard me speak of you, and you have met some of them. Another thing, your program may lead to requests for music lessons, when you are ready to open your studio."

"How kind of you, to give me this opportunity. Let me think, I could sing the semi-classical numbers our Octette learned. And would you like some Spanish songs?"

"Yes, please! And be sure to include one or more of your own compositions," Mrs. Patterson said firmly.

"Come, let's plan your program right now!" Anne said when their neighbor had gone. "Isn't it just too exciting for words!" But as Elizabeth practiced faithfully for the next two weeks, her own moods vacillated from elation to despair. To play and sing before the Woman's Club was a great honor and a marvelous opportunity.

These women could very well hold the key that would open the door to her career! But suppose she failed?

Anne scoffed at her misgivings. "Don't be ridiculous, Gee-Gee. You did it in Austin; you can do it in El Paso."

"I hope you are right. Promise me you will be at my side every minute, though."

"Why? Do you expect to faint or something?" Anne scoffed. "But of course I'll be there. I wouldn't miss it for the world!"

All too soon the momentous day was upon them! They spent anxious moments on their grooming, concentrating first on their hair arrangement. Pompadours were much in fashion, and Anne kept hers puffed high on her head with a "rat", a sort of sausage roll of combings used to pad the pompadour. Some girls were even buying rats made of wire! Her long back hair was braided and coiled and tied with a large bow. Elizabeth preferred her usual braids, which she could manage more easily. Instead of the popular bow, she topped her back braids with a high-backed Spanish comb, creating an individual and extremely attractive effect.

Mrs. Garrett was an expert seamstress. For the past few summers, the girls had dressed in the modest, pretty styles worn by teen-agers of the era. The dresses were snugly belted and the deep yokes of their blousy waists were trimmed with a frill all around. Full braid trimmed skirts reached to mid-calf, and were worn over starched petticoats with crocheted lace edging. Fine-ribbed cotton stockings were visible between skirt and high-topped buttoned shoes.

But this summer, they were suddenly old enough to adopt the popular Gibson girl look. How Mrs. Garrett's needle had flown, turning out new wardrobes! The dresses usually had high collars reinforced with tiny strips of whalebone to make them stand; the waists were more smoothly fitted, and trimmed with rows of lace or braid. The dresses fitted in tight at the belt, then flared out in a bell shape toward the bottom. Now the skirts came to the ankle, and neat dust braids were sewed inside the hem to protect the bottom of the skirt from contact with the shoes. And all young ladies wore tight whalebone corsets, which they laced in to make their waists appear small!

"*Muy bonita!* Very pretty!" Mrs. Garrett nodded her approval as she fastened Elizabeth's high collar at the back with two small enameled pins. Anne was radiant in pink with lace-trimmed ruffles, Elizabeth lovely in white, which accented her sun-kissed coloring and glossy dark hair. Both girls wore white kid buttoned shoes, and each wore a chain and locket.

Mrs. Garrett, too, was fashionably attired in a black lawn

dress of similar style. Her high net collar was fastened with two gold pins. Instead of a locket, she wore a watch fastened to her blouse with a gold *fleur-de-lys* pin. Her black hair was drawn back smoothly into a neat roll, with a highbacked tortoise shell comb securing it. Pompadours were not for her!

"You are ready, now," she said. "*Vaya con Dios, queridas.* I will come later."

As the sisters walked to the Patterson house, Elizabeth's knees were suddenly weak. Her hands trembled. She had never felt like this at school! "I'm nervous, Anne! All those strangers—what will they think of me?"

"Don't bother about that, Gee-Gee; just concentrate on your music. At first, they will only be thinking of how pretty you look, and when you begin to sing, they'll forget everything else!"

Elizabeth squeezed her sister's hand gratefully. She heard murmurs of approval as they entered the reception room, Elizabeth's hand resting lightly on Anne's arm. Her heart surged with love for Anne's constancy and for Madrecita, whose devoted labors provided them with stylish, becoming dresses.

There was a polite flutter of applause after Mrs. Patterson's warm introduction. As Anne escorted Elizabeth to the piano, she saw the tiny beads of perspiration on her sister's forehead. "Just show them now, Gee-Gee, show them!" she hissed in her ear, and was rewarded by a faint but distinct giggle. Anne breathed easier as Elizabeth seated herself at the piano with poise, and the sensitive hands found their place on the keyboard.

"I shall open my program with "La Golondrina," The Dove; and I would like to sing it in my mother's language, Spanish, as it was written," she said.

"Oh Papa, I wish you could have been there!" Anne's dark eyes sparkled as she recounted the events of the afternoon. The family was seated around the big golden oak table for dinner, and for once, Madrecita's superb cuisine was almost forgotten in the excitement.

"The ladies were so kind," Elizabeth said. "I think they really *liked* my music, Papa! They asked for encores, even when I sang my own compositions!"

"And were you there, too, Madrecita?"

"Oh, yes, Pat. I was very proud! But I slipped away early; when I receive such compliments for my daughters I become embarrassed and forget my English. And if I revert to Spanish, then the ladies are embarrassed because they do not understand me! So I came home."

73

Mr. Garrett laughed. "You are a very wise woman, Madrecita."

"And, Papa, the president of the Woman's Club asked Gee-Gee to give a public concert later this summer!" Anne said. "And several ladies said they will call to arrange piano lessons for their children!"

"Well!" Mr. Garrett said in a pleased voice, "it seems you are launched, Elizabeth. Mrs. Patterson has proved to be a good friend and neighbor."

"Elizabeth must have privacy for her lessons," Mrs. Garrett said, as she rose to bring dessert. "The parlor will be her studio. The children never play there, anyway."

"Only for part of the day," Elizabeth said firmly. "I will take pupils for morning hours only. You often have callers in the afternoon, Mama."

"Yes, it is true," Mrs. Garrett sighed. "The people here are very friendly." Mr. Garrett smiled. Because of his position, he met many important officials, both Mexican and American, and the shy, retiring little Madrecita was obliged to entertain in the manner of the day. The bi-lingual Garretts had become very popular as hosts, and had many visitors.

"I overheard the Pattersons talking," Poe said suddenly. "The Judge said Papa is one of the best-known men in the Southwest."

"Well, I am sure of one thing that is more important," Mr. Garrett said. "I am married to the best cook in the southwest."

Family activities soon fell into a pattern. The little boys played in the shady back yard. Mrs. Garrett and Poe supervised the housekeeping. Anne was busy with new friends, and Mr. Garrett, well-groomed and handsome, left the house early each morning for his office in the Customs building.

Several requests for music lessons had followed the concert, and the parlor became Elizabeth's studio during the morning hours. The concert for the Woman's Club was scheduled, as well as engagements for entertainment at other private parties or teas. Elizabeth insisted that Anne act as her escort on these occasions.

"You don't really need me, Gee-Gee," Anne protested.

"I *do* need you, first for moral support. And when others help me they help *too much*. They push me and talk too loud. Some people seem to think a blind person is deaf, too!"

Anne giggled. "People are funny, aren't they? Well, I like the job, I can bask in your reflected glory."

"Silly girl," Elizabeth said fondly. "When you are in school this fall, I shall have to manage, but do stay with me just this summer." Anne consented, pleased.

"I should have a studio, away from the house," Elizabeth said to her father after a few weeks. "I will have more pupils in the fall, and I can't disrupt the household indefinitely. And now that I am earning money, I could pay the rent myself!"

"But you couldn't go there alone," he said, "and Anne will be in school—"

"If it is near our house, I can go and come alone, Papa," she said, "and in between lessons, I can work there on my compositions."

To her delight, Mr. Garrett agreed that they would look for a suitable place. A studio of her own! It would be another dream come true.

Before the fall term of school opened, Mr. Garrett had found it; an airy large room with its own small bathroom. It had been built as a guest house at the back of a neighboring home, but was no longer used. It was large enough to accommodate the precious piano, two comfortable chairs and a table, and shelves to hold Elizabeth's Braille books and equipment. Now she had only to walk down the block and around a corner, with no streets to cross, unlock the door to her studio and her day would begin. At last she was a woman with a career of her own! It was an eminently satisfying arrangement!

"Will you do me a favor, Gee-Gee?" Anne asked one morning. "School will be starting soon, and this is my last chance! Will you go with me to *una vieja*, a little old lady who tells fortunes? There's something I *have* to know!"

Elizabeth smiled. "Of course. We'll go this morning." They found the one-roomed *adobe* house of the little old lady, *la profeta*, who was said to foretell the future with great accuracy!

Anne pushed Elizabeth ahead of her. "You go first, Gee-Gee, while I get my courage up."

"But I only came with you!" Elizabeth protested, but at Anne's insistence, she entered the little house. Several minutes later she returned, wearing a rather quizzical expression. Anne went in, and soon came out with a satisfied air.

"What did she tell you?" Elizabeth asked eagerly.

"Well, she said I have a pleasing voice, but that I have no interest in singing in public! Now how did she know that? And she said I will have a home of my own and a kind husband and lovely children. Just what I wanted to know. And how about you?"

"About my voice, the same as she told you. But she said I will study and travel many miles to large cities and appear before many people. It's amazing, little sister. She told us both just what we wanted to hear!"

Chapter   7

CHAPTER 7

The El Paso period would always be remembered fondly by the Garrett family. It was a happy time, often exciting and sometimes exhausting. But suddenly it was over.

Mr. Garrett's appointment as Collector of Customs was for a four-year term, but he was confident of reappointment. Unfortunately his political advisors had not been aware of the maneuvering taking place for the coveted position.

Without warning, the news broke. Newspapers throughout the Southwest carried the story: Pat Garrett Replaced as U.S. Collector of Customs!

Stunned by this unexpected turn of events, he was faced by the necessity of making immediate plans for his family. Madrecita must be told first of all.

"We will have to move once more," he said. "Back to Las Cruces, I suppose. It isn't fair to you, *querida*, after the hard years when you managed with so little, to be forced now to give up this house and the comforts you deserve."

"The house in Las Cruces is *home*," she said simply. "We don't need a fine house to be happy. Home is where you are, my dearest Pat, you and my children. But what will you do in Las Cruces?"

"I can raise horses again, at least for awhile. A good thing I kept that piece of land east of the Organs." He moved restlessly about the spacious room. "We will have to sell some of your nice furniture, I'm afraid. There won't be room for it all. But we will take what we can, and Elizabeth's piano, of course."

"It will be hard for her to leave El Paso," Mrs. Garrett said slowly, "the other children won't mind at all. But she is happy, and her work is going well."

"I know. I should have looked ahead, Madrecita, I was foolish to depend upon the promises of politicians. But there is nothing for me here now, and we can't leave Elizabeth alone."

Mrs. Garrett's heart ached with sympathy for her husband, although she thought a bit guiltily that for her part, the return to a simple life would be welcome. She had never felt truly comfortable in El Paso's social whirl. How good it would be to visit old friends again, especially Mariana Fountain, who hadn't even seen the two youngest Garrett children! Poor Mariana, she had never fully recovered from the shock and grief caused by the murder of her husband and little son.

"Don't worry, *querido*," she said gently, "our Gee-Gee will understand."

"Aren't you glad we're going back home?" Anne asked her sister late that evening as they were preparing for bed. "You agreed with everything Papa suggested this morning, but I had a feeling you didn't mean it!"

"What about you, Anne? Are you glad to be going?"

"I truly am, Gee-Gee. El Paso has been a marvelous experience, but I really like Las Cruces best."

"I love Las Cruces, too," Elizabeth said slowly, "but the opportunities for me would be limited there. And I have my studio here—I have been thinking all day, and I have a plan!" She paused dramatically. "If Papa and Madrecita will consent, I'm staying right here!"

"You can't!" Anne protested. "You know we have to stay together!"

"But I can! This afternoon I talked it over with Mrs. Patterson. She will let me have a room, she won't miss it in that big house, and my meals, too! She says her cook won't mind. Of course I'll pay, although she says she would like having me whether I pay or not. Isn't she a dear? And I can keep my studio and go on with my work. Just think, Anne, I am self-supporting!"

"Well, it does sound more exciting for you than Las Cruces," Anne admitted, "and more practical, your work here is going so well." She paused, frowning. "But won't you *need me*? I would miss you so, Gee-Gee."

Elizabeth hugged her impulsively. "And I will miss you, dear sister, but I don't want to keep you tied down to me. Just think, we can visit each other, and we will both be busy. As for needing you, of *course* I will often need a companion, but Mrs. Patterson will arrange for an escort when necessary, and I must learn to manage. And oh, Anne! I almost forgot to tell you! I have been offered the position as choir director at the church! Miss Roe sings in the choir, you know."

"The church with the pipe organ! How marvelous! I'm so proud of you, Gee-Gee!"

"Well, I only hope I can do the job well enough! They pay a small salary, too, although I would gladly do it for nothing, to have the privilege of using that organ and directing such a group. Now promise you will help me persuade Papa and Madrecita that I should stay."

Elizabeth was overjoyed when her father approved her plan, even though Madrecita protested at first.

"You said yourself that we can't leave Elizabeth alone," she said tearfully.

"I was wrong, Madrecita. I was forgetting the very thing we

have tried to teach her, to be independent and to learn to carry on without us. We know we can't have our children with us always. Poe is an exception, but Elizabeth is strong and healthy. Her independence is vital."

"And I won't be alone, dear Mama, not when I have my music and my good friends. And the studio! It means so much to be able to let my voice out, full range, to practice my scales, or compose at odd hours without disturbing anyone." And at last Mrs. Garrett agreed.

A few weeks later, when the Garretts were settled again in their modest *adobe* house in Las Cruces, they received a neatly typed letter that reassured them further.

"My lessons are going well," Elizabeth wrote, "and I have two concerts scheduled, one at the Woman's Club, and another at a social affair, a tea in the home of a wealthy lady. The payment isn't large, but it all adds up! A young girl student, who is a protegee of Mrs. Patterson, acts as my companion when I need her. At home or at the studio, I do nicely alone.

"I think I am lucky to be here. It seems that El Paso is growing culturally, and there is a demand for singers, musicians, elocutionists, etc. Thank you, *queridas*, for allowing me to stay."

Mrs. Garrett was deeply thankful. Her children were safe and happy, Elizabeth with her music, Poe occupied on a small scale with his *tortilla* making, Anne busy with school and discovering the joy of romance, Pauline and the three little boys healthy and active.

But as the months passed, she knew her beloved husband was deeply troubled. His business was going poorly, raising horses was proving to be unprofitable. With the growing interest in automobiles there was little demand for the fine carriage horses of former days!

Mrs. Garrett knew, too, that in addition to his financial worries another matter occupied his mind, a rankling obsession he could not dispell; the desire to bring the Fountain murderers to justice.

"Someone will talk," he said, "some day it will all come out. I can wait."

"Oh *querido*!" she protested, alarmed. "It is all past, even Mariana is resigned to her loss. Those men were cruel murderers.

Please do not risk your life again by attempting to expose them!"

"Don't worry, Madrecita. I can take care of myself." He spoke confidently, but an uneasy feeling possessed her each time he left her. His work at the ranch often took him away for days at a time, and her heart was heavy at each parting. The needs of her family pressed upon her, however, and she tried to forget her fears in the routine of her duties.

The tie between Elizabeth and her father had always been strong and tender. At intervals, he called her long distance, not satisfied with only her letters, even though she tried to relate everything that might be of interest to any of the family. But there were always questions he must ask, about her health, her work, social activities and so on, and the telephone provided the means, even though the connection was sometimes poor, long distance telephoning being in its infancy.

On a cold, blustery night in February it was Elizabeth who placed the call. The long conversation that followed began with inquiries about his health and that of Madrecita and the children.

"And what about you, Elizabeth? Are you well?"

"Oh, yes, Papa—I am *very* well," she assured him. "You know I am a healthy girl, as strong as the proverbial horse! By the way, how *are* your horses?"

He chuckled. "My horses are strong enough, it's the market that's weak. Guess I'll have to stock more cattle, if I can get hold of more grazing land. Trouble is, I am not welcome as a neighbor to some of those ranchers, and land is hard to come by. But tell me, how is your work going?"

"Oh, very well, Papa. And of course I am enjoying my work with the choir. I do love that organ!"

Then the question he always asked: "Do you need anything? Extra money?"

"No, thank you, Papa, I'm getting to be quite a business woman. I am even saving a little money!" She sensed relief in his voice, as they continued the conversation which they both were reluctant to bring to a close. At last, after messages to the family and an affectionate good-night, she turned from the telephone. She had thought her father seemed depressed the last few weeks. An unwelcome presentment of impending trouble occupied her mind, and that night her usual sound sleep was disturbed by fitful dreams.

It was loyal Mrs. Patterson who received the message next day with the family's request that she break the tragic news to her young friend. Returning from his ranch alone in the late afternoon, Mr. Garrett had been ambushed and cruelly assassinated!

As she held the stricken girl in her arms, waiting for the first terrible paroxysm of grief to subside, tears of sympathy coursed down her own cheeks. "It is best that you weep, my dear. Weep for your dear father, and for your mother. I understand."

"Oh, my poor Madrecita! My family! How can they go on without Papa? How can I?"

"You are a brave girl, Elizabeth. You have the courage your father always taught you."

"But I am *not* brave at all!" she sobbed. "I am afraid, terribly afraid. Without Papa, I am helpless. I am blind!"

"You must think of your mother," Mrs. Patterson said firmly. "You can help her. She needs you. You must take your father's place."

Elizabeth dried her tears. She sat quietly as Mrs. Patterson's words penetrated her consciousness. How could she take her father's place? She had been able to provide for herself since leaving school, but always with the knowledge that he was near, always ready to come to her aid if she needed him. What did the future hold for her now, and for her dear ones?

Suddenly she recalled the words her father had spoken to a frightened little girl years before: "I know you won't let me down, *querida.*" What had happened to the "courage without fear" he had tried to instill in her? She could not fail him now!

Her ebbing courage began to return. She must go to her family, at least she could comfort them in spirit. She must do what she could; God would do the rest!

Always bound by strong family ties, the stricken Garretts drew even closer in their grief. "Now he is with Ida," Mrs. Garrett wept, as they saw their beloved husband and father laid to rest in the old cemetery in Las Cruces.

In the sad days that followed, Elizabeth tried desperately to comfort her desolated little mother and the bewildered children although her mind was in a turmoil. For the first time she felt the full impact of her handicap. She was determined, however, to keep her misgivings from the others.

There was work to be done, plans to be made. "Must you return to El Paso, to your studio?" Mrs. Garrett asked anxiously.

"No, dear Mama, not to stay. Surely we can find a way, so that we can be together. I have a small amount of money saved, that will tide us over for a time. Why can't I move my piano here, and give lessons at home! Surely I can find a few pupils, and perhaps Anne and I can get some engagements to sing and entertain. Then if I am called upon for a concert in El Paso, I can make the trip by train."

"You would give up the choir?" Anne asked.

Elizabeth shrugged. "That I will regret, of course, but we must be together, at least for awhile. Things will work out, you'll see. Mr. Quesenberry has said he will help you to sell the ranch and the livestock, Madrecita. That will add to our funds."

Her optimism was contagious, and their spirits lifted in spite of their sorrow. It was a brief respite, however, as one discouraging event after another followed. First, it was soon evident that Mr. Garrett's assassin would go unpunished. An itinerant worker who had been employed by the unfriendly neighboring rancher rode into town and gave himself up to the sheriff, stating that he had fired the fatal shot in self-defense, after an argument with the veteran lawman! At the speedy trial that followed, his story was accepted, in spite of the coroner's statement that the victim was shot in the back. The defendant was freed and left the state at once.

When the ranch was advertised for sale, the property was found to be heavily mortgaged. Little would be left after the debts were paid! And after the sale was completed, it seemed a final humiliation that the buyer was an associate of one of the men who had been tried for the Fountain murder. It seemed to the crushed Garrett family that the forces of evil had triumphed completely.

"It was a terrible miscarriage of justice," Mr. Quesenberry said, shocked and deeply disturbed. "It must never happen again. If this catastrophe causes the voters to wake up and elect honest men to office, maybe Pat didn't die in vain."

This seemed small consolation to Elizabeth, as she struggled to find a solution to the problems facing her. Her family was almost destitute, but surely they would be spared the final ignominy of having to accept charity!

She considered returning to El Paso, but she knew her earnings there wouldn't be sufficient for the family needs. Young Pat and Pauline must stay in school, Oscar and Jarvis were still too young for school. Anne had finished high school, but was untrained for work of any kind. She had a good singing voice, but a career didn't interest her.

"Do you know what I really want, Gee-Gee?" she confided. "Maybe I am not very ambitious, but I only want to be married and have a handsome husband and beautiful children!"

"That is a fine career, little sister. I am sure you will realize that ambition."

"What about you? Don't you want a husband and family?"

"I have thought about it, of course," Elizabeth admitted. "I suppose every girl would like a handsome husband and beautiful children—like our dear Mama had. But it may not be intended for everyone. Perhaps not for me."

Sadness welled up in Anne and her eyes filled. "Oh, Gee-Gee, you would make a wonderful wife and mother! Just wait, the right man will come along for you, too!"

"Perhaps." Elizabeth's heart had been so heavy that it came almost as a shock that she could smile at her earnest sister. "Dear Anne, you are good for me! Now, while we wait for your Prince Charming—and mine—we must get busy on a program of songs. We *do* sing well together, surely someone will be asking for our services before long. And I must have my piano shipped right away."

They took the train to El Paso the next day, and with Mrs. Patterson's assistance Elizabeth's books and other possessions were packed and sent along with the treasured piano to Las Cruces. In spite of herself, Elizabeth could not hold back her tears when they walked through the empty studio for the last time. Anne's heart ached with sympathy. "I'm so *sorry*, Gee-Gee, it just isn't fair."

But the tears were swiftly wiped away. "This was my love, my first studio," Elizabeth said sturdily, "and of course I don't like giving it up. But you'll see, Anne, there will be another, and perhaps one even grander!"

Anne breathed a sigh of relief. Elizabeth was herself again. They could depend on Gee-Gee!

As the Garretts faced their problems, the answers slowly appeared. The first of these came when Madrecita discovered that she had an unsuspected earning power. She could work as a practical nurse! But could she bring herself to accept even a modest fee for helping her neighbors? The very idea was distasteful. When friends convinced her, however, that she would be filling a growing need in the community, she agreed, pleased that she could contribute in a small way to the family's finances.

Poe took over the duties of the house, and at times enlisted Anne's help in a catering service, specializing in the delectable Mexican food he prepared so well. His *tortillas* were always in demand, but unfortunately brought a very low price.

Anne was able to work part time in a local dry goods store, as her services with Poe or Elizabeth were usually required only in the evenings. Occasionally the girls were engaged to entertain at social functions, and a few music pupils appeared in response to Elizabeth's notice in the weekly newspaper.

Now the Garretts could manage, by being very careful. Elizabeth realized, however, that her field was too limited, and when she saw her savings dwindling away, she knew she must make other plans. Could the family manage now without her?

Another trip to El Paso and a conference with faithful Mrs.

Patterson and other members of the Woman's Club followed. These sincere friends advised her that further voice training and an enlarged repertoire of songs was necessary if she wished to compete in concert work!

But the finest teachers were far away, in Chicago or New York. "It would be impossible for me," Elizabeth said sadly.

"Wait, let's think about it," one of the women insisted, "it may *not* be impossible! Our music committee has had experience in arranging concerts in El Paso, suppose we expand our field a bit!" And an unbelievable, exciting plan began to take shape.

It was a dramatic moment when she broke the news to her family. "I have news, *queridas*! I am going to leave you for a time. I have decided to go to Chicago to study music. I must have more voice training!"

"Chicago!" Mrs. Garrett exclaimed. "That is so far away! And it would take much money. How could you do it?"

"*Ten fe*, Madrecita! I think a way will be provided. Let's talk it over."

A family conference followed. They discussed the advice her friends in El Paso had given her. Loyally, they agreed that Gee-Gee should go to Chicago. But how?

"Those good ladies have a plan for me, if it will only work," Elizabeth disclosed. "It seems that there is an organization in Chicago called the Young Women's Christian Association. Its purpose is to provide living quarters for young working women who are away from home, at reasonable rates for room and board. They also provide recreation and entertainment, and even have classes in subjects of interest to the girls. There are a certain number of paid employees. Mrs. Patterson wants me to write them, offering my services as an entertainer, musician, teacher, or in any way I could be of use, in exchange for my room and board."

They listened, spellbound. "But you would have to *get* to Chicago, Gee-Gee. You have no money for travel!" Anne said.

"There's more to the plan!" Elizabeth said triumphantly. "The ladies of the Woman's Club are sure this part will work! They say I can *sing* my way to Chicago!"

"How can such a thing be possible?" Mrs. Garrett asked, bewildered by this turn of events.

"There are Woman's Clubs at a few cities en route. My friends will write these clubs, and ask if they are interested in a concert on the date when I will be passing through by train. What do you think, Madrecita? Isn't it a wonderful idea?"

"Suppose they say no?" Poe asked anxiously.

"Then I must find another way, but I think it is important

that I go. Somehow, I must pay my way."

They were silent, thinking. They all knew her savings were gone. "Maybe you could borrow," Poe ventured.

"I'd rather not, even if I could. No, I believe a way will be provided, even a way to earn enough to pay for my lessons when I once reach Chicago. I would like to study with a famous teacher of voice, Dr. Herbert Witherspoon. Oh, *queridas*, I believe I can do it!"

The momentous letters were written, and excitement ran high for days, as they awaited the replies. Bit by bit the good news came: the Woman's Clubs in Wichita, Kansas, Kansas City, and Springfield, Illinois would like Elizabeth's services on the dates suggested. These would be benefit concerts, and she would share the proceeds!

Elizabeth was jubilant; this should more than cover the cost of her fare. "Now if the YWCA can give me something to do—"

At last the letter came from the matron of the Chicago organization. An opening as entertainer and director of music would be forthcoming in the fall, if she wished to accept it. The members of the governing board were pleased with the letters of recommendation they had received from Austin and El Paso.

Now her room and board were assured. The music lessons would come, somehow.

The days passed rapidly now, and soon the time of her departure was imminent. Assisted by Anne, Elizabeth had just finished her packing when the sound of Poe's halting footsteps told Elizabeth he was near. "Come in, Poe," she said. "We're all through packing."

"I have something for you, Gee-Gee," he said shyly. "We know you don't like to borrow, so this is a gift. Here!" he thrust an envelope into her hand. "We think you should have a little extra in your purse when you leave."

With Anne's help, Elizabeth counted the nickels, dimes, quarters, half-dollars and two dollar bills. "Twelve dollars in all!" Anne said proudly. "It's from Madrecita and Poe and me and little Pat, and a few nickels from Pauline. Now don't say you won't accept it!"

Tears welled in Elizabeth's eyes. "My dear, wonderful family, of course I accept it, and I thank you." She laughed shakily. "How did you know I was down to my last ten dollars? Now I will be prepared for an emergency, if one should come up."

"One should always carry a little extra money," Poe said with distinct pride.

El Paso Period. (Blower)

The farm home a few miles east of Roswell where the Pat Garrett
family lived during Elizabeth's early childhood.
(Courtesy of Roswell Historical Museum)

New Mexico Federation of Business and Professional Women's Club — Carlsbad Cavern, May 30, 1933.

Pauline, Elizabeth and friend at San Diego World Exposition –
1915.

Elizabeth Garrett at her piano, about the time of her graduation from the Texas School for the Blind, shortly after the turn of the century.

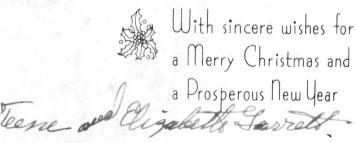

With sincere wishes for
a Merry Christmas and
a Prosperous New Year

Teene and Elizabeth Garrett

Given by Mrs. Norman Blower.

The blue sign of "La Casita" in 1955.

O, Fair New Mexico

Words & Music
BY ELIZABETH GARRETT

Andante

poco rall.

Moderato
with fervor

Un-der a sky of a - zure, Where balm-y breezes blow;
Rug-ged and high si - er - ras, With deep can-ons be - low;
Days that are full of heart-dreams, Nights when the moon hangs low;

Sempre

Kissed by the gold-en sun-shine, Is Nu - e - vo Me-ji-co.
Dot-ted with fer - tile val - leys, Is Nu - e - vo Me-ji-co.
Beam-ing it's be - ne - dic-tion, O'er Nu - e - vo Me-ji-co.

* Mejico - pronounced: Mĕ-hĭ-cŏ.

Copyright,1915, by Elizabeth Garrett.

Home of the Mon - te - zu - ma, With fiery heart a - glow,
Fields full of sweet al - fal - fa, Rich - est perfumes be - stow,
Land with its bright man - a - na, Com - ing through weal and woe,

State of the deeds his - tor - ic, Is Nue - vo Me - ji - co.
State of the ap - ple blossoms, Is Nue - vo Me - ji - co.
State of our es - per - an - za, Is Nue - vo Me - ji - co.

REFRAIN

O, fair New Mex - i - co, We love, we love you so.

Chapter   8

CHAPTER 8

With a hissing of steam and grinding of brakes, the train pulled into the Chicago station. Assisted by the conductor, Elizabeth stepped down onto the crowded platform.

"Thank you very much, you have been most kind," she said. "I can wait here, someone will be meeting me, I am sure."

"Just let me help you out in the crowd a bit, then." He guided her to a less congested spot. "Now, you won't be pushed around quite so badly. Good-bye, Miss, and good luck."

Alone in a crowd, she thought. A trite phrase to most people, but for her, it had a very real significance. In spite of her strong desire to be self-sufficient, the humbling knowledge remained, she must always be dependent upon another person.

She waited, tense and alert, trying to sort out certain familiar sounds in the cacophony that assailed her ears; the grinding of wheels on metal rails, the clanging gongs of passing street cars, and shouts of red caps and taxi drivers. Over all, a continuous muted roar which strangely seemed to come from overhead, accompanied the clacking noise of turning wheels. This must be the elevated train she had read about! The air itself was different, with a cool, damp freshness never experienced in the Southwest. Lake Michigan, that great body of water, must be very near.

Her tension eased at the sound of a voice addressing her: "Miss Garrett? I am Amy Martin, matron at the YWCA. Welcome to Chicago!" Elizabeth's extended hand was taken in a firm, warm clasp.

"How kind of you to meet me!" Elizabeth said.

"Not at all! I could have sent one of the girls, but frankly I was curious! I couldn't wait to meet the young woman who could sing her way to Chicago. And traveling alone, too—I think you must be a brave girl."

"Not brave, just stubborn, maybe," Elizabeth smiled. She liked Mrs. Martin's open, friendly manner, her clipped but well-modulated voice, and the ease with which she guided her charge to a waiting taxicab, after directing a porter to bring the luggage.

"It isn't a long ride," Mrs. Martin said when they were on their way, "but at least we will have a little time to get acquainted. Our building is in the business district, convenient to shops, library, downtown churches, and the business school which some of our residents attend. They are able to walk or take a street car to any place they wish to go. As you know from our correspondence, we have working girls and students in residence, for the most part."

"Girls from out of town?"

"Yes, without exception. Our aim, you know, is to provide a comfortable inexpensive place for young women away from home, in a wholesome, Christian environment. Most of the girls are from small towns or farms, and have come to the city to work or study."

"One could be very lonely in a big city like this," Elizabeth said thoughtfully.

"Yes, lonely and unhappy, and perhaps fall into undesirable company."

"El Paso, Texas, where I have been living since I graduated from school, doesn't have such an organization. Of course it isn't a big city like Chicago. Is the YWCA found only in larger cities?"

"The need is greatest in the large cities, but the movement is spreading. It actually started in England as the Young Men's Christian Association, more than fifty years ago. It was planned to provide a respectable home for young men in London who had come to the big industrial city to work. It was so successful that some years later a similar project for young women was begun here in our country, in Boston. The idea caught on, and now a YWCA can be found in most of the larger cities."

"How fascinating! I must learn more about this wonderful organization!"

"Oh, you'll be hearing much more about the 'Y', as we call it. We have a splendid group of public-spirited men and women who serve on our board, all volunteers. For several years, the original organization had its headquarters here in Chicago, and was known as the American Committee of the YWCA. Now, however, the national board has secured a site and funds for a National Headquarters Building to be erected soon in New York City. Oh, here we are. Driver, will you bring the luggage in, please?"

They walked up a half-dozen steps, through a wide door and into a room that Elizabeth sensed was spacious and airy.

"Our building is brick, and rather large," Mrs. Martin said. "We will give you a detailed description soon. Just now, we will wait here in the main reception hall for a bit." She guided Elizabeth to a comfortable sofa across the room. "The girls who attend business college will be coming in from their classes soon, and one of them, Peggy Johnson, will be your principal companion and escort, with her roommate, Agnes Smith, substituting when needed. Both are delighted with the arrangement you suggested in your letter, that they will be paid for their services by receiving music lessons from you."

"Splendid!" Elizabeth's face brightened. "I truly love teaching music, and especially when the pupils are eager to learn, not just doing it to please their parents, as some I have had!"

"Peggy and Agnes are enthusiastic girls, you'll enjoy them. They are like most of our girls, ambitious and hardworking, looking forward to the time when they can get some kind of job."

Elizabeth's head fairly buzzed with questions. "How many girls are living here?"

"The number fluctuates, usually we have between twenty and thirty, sometimes more. But we have various activities that are open to non-residents, too. We have games and swimming and other recreation, and a number of evening classes in such subjects as cooking, languages, or crafts. Then we have entertainment, and that is where your services to the 'Y' will come in. We consider entertainment important, and for that reason room and board are provided for a qualified director."

"How fortunate for me!" Elizabeth said.

"Something tells me the benefits will be mutual," Mrs. Martin said. "But tell me about your trip, did you have any difficulty?"

"No, everything went quite well. The ladies of the Woman's Clubs were very helpful. At each stop, someone met me. My lodging and an escort to the concerts were arranged for, and they took me to the train next day. My poor mother had many doubts about my coming alone. I must write her at once and tell her she needn't have worried."

"The Woman's Clubs are doing much good work all over the country," Mrs. Martin said. "Woman's suffrage is one worthy cause they are promoting."

"They sponsor most of the cultural events in El Paso," Elizabeth's face glowed with pleasure. "I owe them so much! They gave me my start in concert work, and through them, I learned about Dr. Witherspoon. They encouraged me to come here to study with him, and, as you know, they arranged the engagements en route that made it possible."

"I am told Dr. Witherspoon is a fine musician," the older woman said, "but aren't his lessons very expensive?"

"I'm afraid so," Elizabeth said, ruefully, "but somehow I must manage that part, too. I hope to find work, during my spare time."

"Teaching?"

"No, I would need a private studio for that, and I can't afford it. But I should like to sing, for special occasions such as weddings, funerals, private teas or parties—possibly play or sing in restaurants during the dinner hour. I have done these things both in Austin and El Paso."

"Well! Such ambition should be rewarded!" Elizabeth

warmed to the approval in the matron's voice. "Perhaps we can help you with some contacts."

Just then the street door opened, and the quiet of the room was broken by a chatter of voices as several girls entered.

"Girls!" Mrs. Martin called. "Come over and meet our newcomer. This is Elizabeth Garrett, our musician and entertainer. First, Elizabeth, you must know Peggy Johnson and Agnes Smith, your roommates."

Elizabeth rose and extended her hand, which was taken in a friendly clasp by each girl in the group as they were introduced. She listened attentively as each voiced a cordial greeting, sensing that the girls had been well prepared by the efficient matron for their "different" guest.

"I will leave you now," Mrs. Martin said. "Peggy and Agnes will show you your room, and take you on the grand tour of our building."

"First, you must tell me *how* I can help you," Peggy said.

"Just let me take your arm, until I know my way around," Elizabeth was pleased with the girl's direct approach.

"Here we go, then, up a flight of stairs. They are wide, and not too steep. All the sleeping rooms are on the upper floors. You will have a small private room next to ours, and you will share a connecting bathroom with Agnes and me. Now please tell us when and just how we can be of assistance; you see, we haven't had any similar experience—"

"Thank you, I *will* tell you. But after I am familiar with the stairs and the arrangement of the rooms and the rest of the building, I won't need much help, except when I go out."

"Mrs. Martin *said* this would be true, but we couldn't believe it!" Agnes exclaimed. "We talked it over, wondering how you could do it. We would close our eyes and try to find our way about but ended up with nothing but bruises!"

Elizabeth laughed. "You would learn! Of course, it is second nature to me, I have always used my other senses to the fullest, to compensate for lack of sight. I must see with my hands, my ears, even my nose is a help!"

They watched in amazement as her hands moved deftly over the bed, dresser, and chairs in her room. She learned that her closet door was directly opposite the bathroom she would share with them. "I should unpack right away," she said, "while it's all fresh in my mind." Unaided, she opened her suitcases and hung her dresses, jackets and coats in the closet. Then she sorted other articles of clothing and placed them in dresser drawers and finally arranged her toilet articles in a cabinet allotted to her in the bathroom.

"Such an assortment of colognes and perfumes!" Agnes exclaimed. "No wonder you smell so good!"

Elizabeth laughed. "My sister Anne and I have a weakness for perfumes, I'm afraid. We lived just across the border from Mexico for a few years, and we could buy marvelous French perfume in Juarez at very reasonable prices. I couldn't resist bringing these, although of course I can't use it all myself! Please let me share them with you!"

"Wow! What a sweet-smelling trio we'll be!" Peggy said, greatly pleased. "Perfume is high on the list of things I would love but can't afford! Along with voice lessons. You're bringing us luck, Elizabeth."

"I think I'm the lucky one! Now please tell me about *you*, your voices have told me a lot, but I must know just how you look!"

"Oh!" Agnes faltered in mock consternation. "I am happy to tell you Peggy is a beautiful, slender blue-eyed blond, but do you *have* to know that I am fat and freckled and have red hair that refuses to stay put?"

"Don't believe her, Elizabeth," Peggy laughed, "she isn't really fat, just *curvy*, which is much better than being a sort of bean pole, like me. And I'm *not* beautiful."

"I think you are *both* beautiful!" Elizabeth said with such emphasis that her companions giggled.

"You'll turn our heads, —dear Miss Garrett," Agnes said. "We'd better follow instructions, now, and show you around the place or Mrs. Martin will have us on the carpet."

An unhurried tour of the entire building followed. Elizabeth was guided down the stairs again, through the main reception room into the library, the dining hall and kitchen, the staff offices, and last, the large recreation room, which the girls explained held tables and chairs for games or handwork.

"Now *this* end of the room is really fun!" Peggy said. "We have a marvelous new phonograph here on this table . . ." Elizabeth's hands moved swiftly over the big horn. "And on these shelves, at the side, are our records! We have some of Caruso's, one of Galli-Curci, and several—"

"Galli-Curci!" Elizabeth breathed. "Oh, some day I must hear her sing! I have been told she *may* come to Chicago!"

"I hope so!" Peggy said. "To hear a great singer like that—"

"And here is the piano," Agnes broke in. "Now *I* want to hear the great pianist, Paderewski, when he comes here next month! If I can save enough money—"

102

Elizabeth's hands caressed the piano keys. Her thoughts were racing ahead . . . to play this piano, to sing and play for these new friends, to teach them what she knew, to attend the concerts where the great talents of the musical world would be heard—her head was spinning with excitement!

"If I can save enough money to attend the concerts," Agnes was saying, "I won't miss a one!"

"Yes, concerts cost money," Elizabeth thought ruefully of the few dollars remaining in her purse. "*Ten fe*, Elizabeth," she said to herself. There must be a way, if one had faith.

Elizabeth was increasingly grateful for the valuable experience the El Paso years had given her. With Mrs. Martin's cooperation, a satisfactory schedule was worked out. During the morning hours, the recreation room was available for her own practice, with lessons for Peggy and Agnes arranged at an early hour, before the girls left for business school.

In the afternoons, she played the piano for ballet and acrobatic dance classes, folk singing and dancing, or other activities sponsored by the "Y." Many non-residents took advantage of these classes. Elizabeth loved sharing the joys of music and expression, and she was doubly rewarded by the eagerness and enthusiasm of the girls.

On regularly planned nights, she sang and played for the entertainment of the resident girls and visitors. Other evenings were spent in informal group singing or listening to records.

Mrs. Martin was highly pleased with her next report to the board. The new director of entertainment was working out very well! She knew there had been misgivings. It was difficult for some members to envision a blind person in such a position.

El Paso friends had written Dr. Witherspoon and the time approached when Elizabeth would visit his studio for the interview he had arranged.

"He may not accept me as a student," she confided to her roommates and Mrs. Martin, "after he hears me sing!" The girls were horrified at such a possibility.

"But you came all this distance to study with him!" Peggy cried. "What would you do?"

Elizabeth shrugged. "The school has other excellent teachers. I would be assigned to one of them, I suppose. Of course I would be horribly disappointed, but I was told before I came that he takes only a limited number of students, now that he goes to New York for the opera season."

They knew that the distinguished young singer was already launched on an auspicious career, although only in his early thirties.

A graduate of Yale University, he had studied singing and acting abroad, and had toured as soloist with several leading American orchestras. Now associated with the Chicago Musical College, he spent several weeks in New York each winter, where he sang first basso with the Metropolitan Opera Company.

On a crisp October morning, three excited young women appeared at the music studio, and after a brief wait, were shown into Dr. Witherspoon's quarters. Seized with shyness in the presence of the dynamic musician, Agnes remained flushed and speechless, but Peggy steeled herself to a semblance of poise, and managed the introductions. Elizabeth stood with quiet dignity, her hand slightly extended. She liked his firm hand clasp, and his pleasant greeting that helped to put them at ease. But it was the beautiful, vibrant voice that dominated her consciousness.

"Now, young ladies," he addressed the nervous escorts, "will you leave your friend here for an hour? We must talk about a number of things, and perhaps Miss Garrett and I will sing a few notes for each other."

Elizabeth took a deep breath. The long-awaited moment had come. The important decision would soon be made. How could she sing for this distinguished teacher? She was sure nothing more than a dismal croak would emerge from her paralyzed throat!

Years later, she would remember with gratitude the kindness of this great man, whose genius and fame did not prevent an innate understanding and sympathy for others. As he questioned her with geniune interest, her misgivings were forgotten. They discussed her musical training at the Austin school, and her launching as a teacher, entertainer, and choir director in El Paso. He listened attentively to her explanation of the use of Braille for musical notations.

"Now if you will stand here by the piano, we will sing a bit," he said. "What shall it be? An aria, or something on the lighter side—what would you like to sing?"

"'Un Bel Di' from Madam Butterfly?" she flushed. "But perhaps Puccini is too ambitious a choice. I could sing Murdock's 'My True Love Lies Asleep' or something of Cadman's, or 'Franchonette', by Clarke—"

"Good! Let's begin with 'Franchonette'." He played a few bars, then sang alone, then asked her to sing with him. "Now take it alone," he said.

In the joy of singing, she forgot that she was on trial. The pure notes poured forth as she sang the familiar air with ease and confidence. Without comment, when the song was ended, he began the opening bars of "Un Bel Di." "Go ahead, please. Let me hear it." It was one of her favorite arias, and she sang it with pleasure.

"You have a good voice, Miss Garrett, well worth developing further," he said rising from the piano. "I shall be happy to take you for a weekly lesson, at this same time, shall we say? Except, of course, for the weeks when I must be in New York for the opera season."

In a daze of happiness, she thanked him; then remembered to ask about the rates.

"You may arrange payment with the secretary in the business office," he said, taking her arm and opening the door to the anteroom. "I see your friends are waiting. Au revoir, then ladies, until next week."

One look at Elizabeth's radiant face told Peggy and Agnes what they were waiting to hear: the visit had been successful! "Take me to the business office, please," she said proudly. "I must arrange payment for my lessons."

The fee was greater than she had expected, several times more than she had ever received for a lesson! Nonplussed, she hesitated. Suppose she couldn't meet the payments? But she dare not let this opportunity pass! The privilege of being tutored by this talented teacher was truly beyond price. Through him she would learn from the great masters of New York, London, Paris and Munich with whom he had studied.

Grateful and humble, she paid for her coming lesson. What matter that only a few dollars remained in her purse! She would find a way to fill it again!

Dr. Witherspoon and his wife, known professionally as Florence Hinkle, were in demand for concert appearances, and were especially noted as oratorio singers. Elizabeth rarely missed their performances, and one or both roommates were always eager to accompany her.

"Tell me about the Witherspoons," she begged her friends. "I must know how they look! I know Dr. Witherspoon is tall, and his voice has its own personality, just as Miss Hinkle's does. But tell me more."

"Yes, Dr. Witherspoon is tall, probably six feet two," Peggy began.

"Tall, like my father," Elizabeth said. "Does he have dark hair and blue eyes, too?"

"No, his hair and moustache are sort of sandy color, and his eyes are gray, I think. He wears glasses, and he has a studious, sort of stately, look."

"They say he looks British," Agnes joined in. "His wife is

tall and slender, too, and light in coloring."

Elizabeth's admiration and respect for her instructor grew as busy weeks passed. She knew that her voice was greatly improved, the reward for hours filled with work, lessons, breathing exercises and practice. She managed to sandwich in pleasant hours of recreation, too, with her friends. They made tours of the city and took boat rides on Lake Michigan, always carefully hoarding their money for the supreme treat of attending operas and concerts.

Through Mrs. Martin she had secured several engagements as entertainer during the dinner hour in a few select restaurants, where her Spanish and Mexican songs were particularly well received. On these occasions she liked to wear one of the colorful handmade dresses she and Anne had shopped for in Juarez. The costume her roommates liked best, however, was a dress of delicate white fabric with many dainty hand-embroidered ruffles, worn with a fringed white silk Spanish shawl embroidered lavishly with red roses. A high-backed comb of silver filigree topped her coronet of shining dark braids.

"This costume is *you*, Elizabeth," Peggy said with enthusiasm. "You look so romantic, so Spanish! The white dress and red roses complement your ivory skin and dark eyes *perfectly*!"

"Please, you'll make me vain!" she remonstrated. "You are dears, though, to help me with my appearance. It does give me confidence, to know that I am suitably dressed."

The restaurant engagements paid modest fees and were welcome, but through the Witherspoons and the studio, requests for private appearances began to trickle in. An hour's entertainment in a private home usually meant a five dollar bill, and sometimes an exciting ten!

A noted singer was coming to Chicago, singing the role of Violetta in the opera, La Traviata. "Dr. Witherspoon urged me to hear her," Elizabeth said. "We simply *must* go!"

"But the tickets are expensive, can we afford it?" they asked anxiously.

"Well, seats in the upper balconies are much cheaper than orchestra seats, and Miss Hinkle assured me we can hear very well. She says real music lovers don't care *where* they sit."

"I know the story of the opera," Peggy said, "it is terribly sad, with poor Violetta wasting away and dying, I know I shall weep *buckets* of tears! You're right, Elizabeth, we must go!"

Their tickets were for third balcony. When the long awaited evening arrived, they were seated a full thirty minutes early, with her companions on either side of Elizabeth. They murmured excited descriptions of the great opera house, its magnificent crystal chandeliers, and the elegantly dressed people in the boxes and main floor seats. Occupants of the crowded balconies were in less formal attire.

"The lights are dimming!" Agnes whispered, and abruptly the rustlings and murmurings of the crowd subsided. A hush fell over the audience, as the first haunting notes of the overture swept through the great hall. The girls sat entranced by the indescribable sounds of violins, wood instruments and brass blending and swelling in exquisite harmony.

When the soloist began the aria replete with sorrow and lamentation, a slight nudge from Agnes roused Elizabeth from a state of hypnotic concentration. "Spread this over your lap," came a whisper, "you will be prepared." Puzzled, Elizabeth felt of the object moving over her knees. It was a roller towel, which could surely take care of the most copious buckets of tears! With an effort, she and Peggy silenced the giggles that threatened. Their composure restored, they settled back to enjoy the thrilling experience of hearing for the first time the superb orchestration and magnificent voices of a great opera.

There were times when Elizabeth could hardly believe her good fortune. To study with Dr. Witherspoon, to hear the great music of the world rendered by its finest artists, and to earn her living by doing work she enjoyed—what more could she ask?

One day, however, a long letter from Anne brought on an acute attack of homesickness. All was well at home, but she was missed. When would she be coming home? Bettie, now busy teaching first graders, had asked about her. Bettie also had a romantic interest! And Anne had part time work, but it was apparent that her greatest interest was a young man who had become very attentive.

Nostalgia swept over Elizabeth. She had a few dollars saved, enough to pay her fare home. She was better prepared now to resume her concerts in El Paso and other towns, and she could be near her beloved family.

She slept poorly that night, as she struggled with these tempting thoughts. When morning came, her practical nature came to the rescue. Dr. Witherspoon had told her she should have at least two years of study. Only half of the time had passed, and her position at the "Y" was assured for another year. It would be sheer folly to leave Chicago now.

"Just a few more months, *querida*," she wrote Anne, "and I will be going home. I long for the day to come! Write often, dear sister, and give me all the news. I miss you all, so much, but my work here is not finished."

Chapter 9

CHAPTER 9

The year was 1912, a time of rejoicing for all the people of New Mexico. On January 6, President Taft signed the bill which officially admitted the Territory of New Mexico to the Union as the forty-seventh state, more than sixty years after its beginning in 1851!

Las Cruces was much the same; a small, sleepy village with dusty streets lined with brown *adobe* houses, each set in its own small oasis. The gardens behind patio walls were still fed by little ditches, and in summer roses, lilacs and sweet peas flourished, perfuming the air.

On a warm June evening, the Saturday night moving picture show was about to begin. Entertainment in the small town was hard to come by, and the weekend "movie," with music furnished by an electric player piano, always drew a packed house.

But suddenly the theater was plunged into darkness, as a summer thunderstorm put the town's electricity out of commission. A murmur of disappointment followed the manager's announcement that the show would be postponed, and the audience prepared to leave, guided by the weak glow of an usher's flashlight. Then a voice was heard, above the rustling of the crowd, a rich, melodious voice that commanded attention.

"Would you like some music? I should be happy to sing for you."

Elizabeth Garrett! Many knew that voice, and enthusiastic applause welcomed her, as Anne and the usher escorted the singer to the piano.

For the next hour, the lovely voice poured forth in the darkness. Playing her own accompaniment, she sang popular western cowboy songs, haunting ballads of old Mexico sung in her faultless Spanish, an aria from an opera in Italian, and finally, several of her own compositions: songs of orchards and gardens, apple blossoms and roses; of the mountains and valleys of her homeland. There was something for every taste, and the darkness was forgotten.

Elizabeth had come home with a distinct sense of pride in her state and a welcome feeling of belonging. "We've grown up together, my New Mexico and me," she said.

"Listen to this editorial!" Anne was looking through the El Paso paper.

"We share the joy of our neighbors in the achievement of statehood at last. There is no doubt that the ruthless murder of a dedicated man of the law a few years ago stirred the citizenry to action, and brought about long needed reforms in election procedures and choice of candidates. Perhaps the family of Pat Garrett may find some consolation in this."

"If only Papa could know!" Elizabeth said sadly. "If only he might have lived to see some of his dreams come true."

Elizabeth was happy to be reunited with her family, and to visit the Quesenberrys again. Plans for Bettie's approaching wedding usually dominated the conversation, although Mr. Quesenberry often spoke of the great dam under construction at last on the Rio Grande seventy-five miles to the north. He explained that a large lake would be formed, storing the water to irrigate thousands of acres of valley land, and providing a fine recreational area for boating, swimming and fishing; a welcome bonus in the semi-arid country. And valuable crops would soon replace the cactus and sage and mesquite.

Elizabeth made a new acquaintance that summer who would become another of her devoted friends. May Rees was a young teacher in the public school where little Jarvis was one of her first grade pupils, and to her delight, a most helpful translator for the children who spoke no English. A newcomer to the state, May was fascinated by its history and intrigued by her neighbors, the indomitable Garretts.

Anne had willingly resumed her duties as Elizabeth's escort, but they knew this arrangement must be temporary. Anne was in love! Her wedding would follow Bettie's by only a few weeks. So May Rees became her substitute during the vacation weeks, a most agreeable arrangement, as the two budding career women discovered many mutual interests.

The Las Cruces Woman's Club, supported by civic minded individuals and following the example of their El Paso neighbors, was now sponsoring cultural events. Taking pride in their talented native daughter, they arranged concerts for her throughout the new state.

One community leader, a music lover and a bachelor, was the owner of a general merchandise store where Anne worked on occasion. A man of dignified bearing, he was known as "the Major," as he had served as an officer in the Spanish-American war.

One day Anne, who was usually moving in a romantic, dream-like mood, came home in a high state of excitement.

"Gee-Gee! I have a message for you! An important message!"

"My, you *are* excited, little sister. Quick, tell me! What is this important message?"

"The Major! He asks your permission to come calling!"

"The Major! Your employer?"

"Oh, yes, Gee-Gee. He is such a fine person, and so *distinguished* looking, and he *loves* music. Gee-Gee, maybe he is *your* Prince Charming!"

Elizabeth laughed. "Many people love music, Anne dear. But not many men could love a blind singer."

"Oh, Gee-Gee!" Anne remonstrated. "Any man in his right mind could love you!"

"Here we go, jumping to conclusions! After all, the poor man has only asked to call. He probably only wants to discuss music. Even so, I'm not sure that I should have him come. Gossip starts so easily."

"Oh, do see him, Gee-Gee. He says he has never heard a voice as beautiful as yours!"

"How could I refuse a visit from such a man?" Elizabeth smiled. "One thing is certain, he has an enthusiastic advocate!"

At first, Elizabeth found the Major's visits extremely pleasant. He had received his education in eastern schools and had heard many of the great singers of opera and stage. His love for music and his deep regard for the southwest and its people created an immediate bond between them.

She liked the drives down country lanes in his fringed-top surrey on long summer evenings, delighting in the fragrance of newly mown hay or the pungent scent of greasewood and sage after a summer shower, when the fresh, cool air quickened the senses.

She listened eagerly to his description of his proud-stepping carriage horses. "I still miss the farm life we enjoyed as children," she confided. "I learned to love horses, just as my father did. One of my earliest memories is the feel of rhythm and power in my pony's rippling muscles as I rode him bareback about the barnyard. I loved all the animals, but especially the kittens, puppies, calves and ponies—they were so responsive to love and care! But the baby ducks and chickens were fun, too. We even had guineas, and cunning, downy babies they were, but I must admit I didn't like their raucous voices when they grew up, until I learned that they provided an efficient alarm system for their friends, warning them of marauding hawks or other enemies. Oh!" she stopped suddenly. "I must be boring you!"

"Quite the contrary," he assured her. "Please tell me more about your early impressions." He was fascinated by the sensitive face and expressive voice, which changed with every mood.

"The farm was a joy-filled world for me," she continued. "I remember my delight in the fragrance of alfalfa fields and apple orchards, the hum of bees, the supple boughs of trees I climbed, the bird calls I learned to imitate—nothing escaped my ears, or my nose! The pleasant smells I remembered, the others I tried to forget, although of course they were a part of my education, too."

He was amazed to find that she could recognize the variety and color of a rose by its fragrance. He learned that the scent of white roses pleased her most of all, and whenever possible, he brought a bouquet of white roses when he came to call.

Suddenly, however, the visits ended. Anne was mystified. "What has happened, Gee-Gee? Is the Major away?"

"No, I am truly sorry, but the pleasant interlude had to end. He asked me to become his wife!"

"Well, of course! I was sure he would propose. And how I hoped you would accept, Gee-Gee. A home of your own, someone to care for you, children—"

"Ah, yes, dear sister, it is a beautiful dream! I must admit to you, in confidence, that I was tempted. A home of my own, economic security, opportunities for travel and entertaining, it would be the easy path, attractive at first glance."

"Then why *not*?"

Elizabeth sighed. "The Major is a fine gentleman and an interesting companion, but as you know, there is a considerable difference in our ages. I believe a marriage should be based on more than the material things." She paused. "Maybe I was looking for a protector, a *father*—someone to take Papa's place. Would such an arrangement be fair? And if I should have children, could they be happy with a mother who is blind? Yes, I can say that forbidden word now with no bitterness. I am blind! But I am independent, and my greatest wish is now as it has always been, that I will never become a burden to anyone."

"You would never be a burden!" Anne cried. "The Major knows how self-sufficient you are. You would make a wonderful wife and mother!"

"Thank you, dear Anne. But I have made up my mind. Music is my life, and I cannot exchange creativity for ease, although the idea was attractive for a time. But I must soon have a place of my own, where I can work at my music at three or four o'clock in the morning if the mood strikes me; where, during daytime hours I can continue with giving lessons or friends can drop in to visit. How could any marriage withstand such a routine? No, I'm afraid marriage is not for me."

So Anne's effort at matchmaking ended, and she soon forgot

her disappointment in plans for her own wedding to handsome young John Montgomery.

Elizabeth made frequent trips to El Paso, giving concerts or visiting with her friend, the "other Elizabeth." They often talked of a trip they must make to New York, to hear the great artists who appeared there during the opera season.

"As soon as we can afford it, we should go for a year, at least."

"A year in New York! It would be a wonderful experience," Beth agreed. "We must save our money!"

Ominous rumors of war in Europe became reality in 1914, when the German Kaiser ordered troops into Belgium. *It can't happen here*, Americans said, reassuring each other. To the people of the Southwest, far removed from the eastern seaboard, Europe and its problems seemed remote, indeed.

Returning from a concert tour in Arizona in the early spring, Elizabeth was met at the depot by young Pat, now a tall, slender youth of eighteen.

"I am flattered that my busy brother could take the time to meet me," she said fondly. She knew that in addition to his studies at the college he was reading law books in the office of a leading attorney in Las Cruces.

"Well, all the others were busy, and I had no classes this afternoon." He took her suitcase in one hand and linked his free arm in hers, matching her stride easily as they walked up the quiet street toward the Garrett house. "And then I am curious about something. You have some mail waiting, and I couldn't help noticing that one letter is from the Governor!"

"From Governor McDonald?" Of course Pat would be intrigued; he shared her pride in their heritage and was already interested in the politics of their new state. But she, too, was curious. Why would the Governor write to her?

The puzzle was soon solved. The letter contained an exciting invitation: Would Miss Garrett represent the State of New Mexico at the coming World's Fair, the San Diego Exposition? Her chief duty would be to present a program of song and entertainment daily in the New Mexico building. At other times, she would act as official hostess to visitors. An escort of her own choosing would be provided.

"Oh, Pat! What a wonderful honor, to represent my dear New Mexico! I could shout for joy!"

"Try singing instead, you'll need the practice," he said mischievously. "You'd better write the Governor at once, before he changes his mind."

"Oh, I shall! I shall! And I must think about an escort, Pat! Why couldn't you go with me? You've never been to California, nor have I. What a fine summer we could have!"

"I only wish I could," he said. "But I'm afraid I can't spare the time. Studying in Judge Young's law office is valuable experience for me. You see," she sensed the pride in his voice, "I am planning to go into the diplomatic service."

"How exciting! Why, that would mean living abroad, at least part of the time, wouldn't it! I am very proud of you, little Pat."

"Little Pat, indeed! I'm taller than you, Gee-Gee."

She shook her head. "It can't be possible! It seems only yesterday that you were a baby! I am happy about your wonderful plans, Pat. We really do live in a land of opportunity, don't we. If one is willing to work, and sets a goal, the way appears."

"You're right, Gee-Gee, we do live in a great country. Now about your escort, why not ask your alter ego?"

"Beth! She would be perfect, and I'm sure she'll do it!"

"Of course she will, it's inevitable, the way things work out," Pat laughed. He couldn't resist teasing her, but her optimism and enthusiasm were happily contagious. "You know, Gee-Gee, you are living proof of your own philosophy," he added more seriously. "I think you should know that you are an inspiration to this family."

"Just as you are to me, each one of you, dear Pat," she said, giving him a warm hug. "Now I must get at the letters, the first to Governor McDonald, and another to Beth. On second thought, I think I should call her on the telephone tonight!"

"This is like a tropical paradise, compared to our arid country," Beth Roe exclaimed. "Tropical in appearance, but cooled by these delightful ocean breezes!"

They were spending their first hours in San Diego exploring the unique city. Elizabeth listened intently to her companion's careful descriptions of the buildings, predominantly of Spanish Mediterranean architecture, with sparkling white walls and red-tiled roofs, and the wide streets lined with tall palm trees. They walked through verdant, well-kept parks with lush, flowering shrubs and plants of every conceivable hue, and visited mission churches where the early Spanish influence was so charmingly preserved. And everywhere, Elizabeth's insatiable curiosity led her to taste, touch, sniff as she sorted out her impressions of this delightful place.

They tried the sea food restaurants near the wharf, and sometimes walked barefoot on the clean, sandy beaches or sat quietly on the shore listening to the mysterious sounds of the waves as the tide came in. "I can see several large ships in the harbor!" Beth said. "The fleet is in! We should have known, from the number of sailors on the streets."

"I have heard that tours are arranged at times, for visits to one of the battleships," Elizabeth said, ever eager for new experiences. "We must look into it."

They took an apartment a few blocks from the Exposition grounds, and in a few days they were established as official hostesses in the Spanish-styled New Mexico building. Colorful displays of Indian pottery, handmade baskets and beadwork, and handsome handwoven rugs attracted many visitors.

The daily program of entertainment drew enthusiastic crowds. At this period Beth assumed the duty of hostess, while Elizabeth, playing her own accompaniment, presented the songs of old Mexico, cowboy ballads, and Indian chants. She closed with a group of her compositions which told of mountains and valleys and apple orchards, of summer showers on mesa and desert, the beauty of the stately yucca, and the antics of the little clown, *Piasano*, the roadrunner; her own songs of New Mexico.

One day stood out above all others. Elizabeth was asked to plan a special program to honor a noted visitor, Colonel Theodore Roosevelt, former President of the United States! Returning from a good will mission to South America, he would be accompanied by a group of distinguished political figures from the countries he had visited.

At the close of the program members of the entourage thanked her for the entertainment she had provided. "Your music is pure Castillian," the Spanish-speaking officials agreed warmly, thus bestowing their highest accolade!

"It is a great pleasure to meet the daughter of my old friend, Pat Garrett," Colonel Roosevelt said. His hand clasp was strong and firm, his voice hearty and confident, the voice of a dynamic, outgoing man, as Elizabeth would have expected. "Miss Garrett's father was the most noted sheriff of the Southwest, in territorial days," he explained to his companions, as Elizabeth's heart warmed with pride. "In fact, I feel that he was the man who *introduced* law to the territory."

When the exciting days of the Exposition came to a close, the two Elizabeths returned home a bit reluctantly, but with a happy feeling of pride and accomplishment.

"It will be hard to settle down to the routine of a school teacher's existence," Beth mused as their train sped over the miles toward El Paso. "Gee-Gee, I am about ready to take a leave of absence from teaching. We should make that trip to New York!"

"We should!" Elizabeth agreed. "To hear some great operas, to visit that greatest of all cities, perhaps to study again with a fine teacher—"

"We must save every penny this year!" Beth said determinedly. "We will build up our bank accounts, and next year, we will go."

Filled with plans for the future, they plunged into their work again. Elizabeth found a number of engagements waiting, and her loyal friends of the Woman's Clubs ever ready to provide her with an escort when needed.

The year 1916 saw increasing growth in the new state of New Mexico and the long awaited completion of Elephant Butte Dam. The years of labor and dreams were at last bearing fruit. Now truly the desert began to bloom like the rose!

Elizabeth's pride in her state bubbled over into song, a song which could only have one title: *O Fair New Mexico*!

Governor McDonald had been highly pleased at the reception given to New Mexico's "First Lady of Song" at the San Diego Exposition. In appreciation, he extended an invitation to Elizabeth to visit his home in Santa Fe, the capitol, and to sing before the legislature.

"I must sing my Fair New Mexico for them," she told Anne. "But first you must listen and criticize. It must be just right."

Anne, now a busy housewife and proud mother of a little son, agreed to act as critic.

"It is a lovely song, Gee-Gee," she said, when she heard it the first time. "But isn't it difficult for the average voice? The key is rather high."

"Perhaps, a little," Elizabeth said thoughfully. "But I think it must be written that way. To me, that key expresses the grandeur of the high mountains, deep canyons, and wide valleys. I shall explain that to my listeners in Santa Fe."

When the appointed day arrived, she sang her song freely and for the joy of singing, to a joint session of the legislature. To her amazement and delight, she learned next day, that the body voted unanimously to make *O Fair New Mexico* the official state song.

"It is a fitting tribute to a great native daughter of a great new state," the Governor said. "A competent music critic who heard it has said that with its Spanish rhythm it stands out in unique beauty above any state song."

This happy period in Elizabeth's life was overshadowed when in 1917 the United States entered the war which was raging in Europe. Many homes were saddened when American troops shouldered their guns and marched away to train for battle in a foreign land. One of these was Bettie's brother, Joseph. Young Pat Garrett did not enter military service, as he had applied for a position as secretary in the American Embassy in Rome.

Mrs. Garrett and Pauline did their part in the local Red Cross projects, and Elizabeth plunged into busy days of entertaining the soldiers in training camps and hospitals throughout the Southwest.

"Your contribution is especially valuable," she was told by the commander of the large military post at Fort Bliss, on the outskirts of El Paso. "These men need laughter and hope. Your optimism and cheerful outlook, despite your handicap, has a healing influence on these men who are often discouraged, sick in body and spirit."

After one of these programs, the two Elizabeths came to a momentous decision. They had learned that there were many training camps on the east coast, and the hospitals were filled not only with the ill, but many returning wounded from the battlefields of France and Belgium. They had been informed that the Red Cross would welcome Elizabeth's services further afield.

In a flurry of excitement, they made their plans to go to New York, and Beth resigned her teaching position to become her friend's traveling companion.

Elizabeth returned to Las Cruces to arrange her business affairs and take leave of family and friends. Once more the family gathered about the table to enjoy the good meal Poe had prepared. "The work for the Red Cross is highly rewarding," she told them, "but I am being a bit selfish, too. I will have an opportunity for further study and to hear good operas. I may even hear the famous Galli-Curci again!"

Anne solemnly reminded her of the little old fortune teller, *la profeta*, whose predictions were coming true. Surely *la buena ventura* was now in Elizabeth's grasp, and Anne's happiness was assured. "She certainly told it as it was to be, for both of us, Gee-Gee."

Pat announced that he also would be leaving soon. "Mr. Young says they need competent secretaries over there, and he thinks I'll do."

"Oh, take me with you!" Pauline exlaimed, brown eyes sparkling.

"I wish I could! Maybe sometime later, when this war has ended."

Madrecita bustled about, waiting on her sons and daughters. Long ago she had ceased to be surprised at anything the venturesome Elizabeth decided to do. And now Pat, too, would be going far away. But that was what she wanted for her children, to be active, ambitious and happy.

A week later, the two Elizabeths were on an east bound train. En route, one stop would be made in San Antonio, where Elizabeth Garrett would sing for thousands of soldiers in the immense army camp located there. The next stop would be for a brief stay in the fascinating city of New Orleans, solely for rest and diversion and to explore the culinary delights for which the city was famous. After a few days there, they would board the ship that would take them to their final destination, New York!

Chapter 10

CHAPTER 10

The ship carried a cargo of food and other supplies vital to the war effort, along with a reduced number of passengers. From New Orleans, it followed the coastal route around the Gulf of Mexico to the southernmost tip of Florida, then up the Atlantic coast to New York harbor. German submarines had been sighted in these waters, and the ship, proceeding with utmost caution, was blacked out nightly.

No entertainment of any kind had been arranged for the voyage, but passengers accepted the restrictions of wartime with good grace. However, the dismal lounges and equally somber thoughts of lurking submarines cast an aura of gloom over the first evening at sea and provided an immediate challenge to the two Elizabeths.

On the following evening they suggested an impromptu musical program. The Captain consented readily. "Anything to keep up the morale of our crew and the passengers," he said. "We should invite all on board, except those engaged in active duty. But can you manage with very little light?"

Elizabeth laughed. "I won't need light; just a piano, and of course, an audience!"

The darkened lounge was crowded with passengers, ship's officers, and crew. Elizabeth started with the ever-popular western and Mexican songs, then filled several requests for favorite ballads and sacred songs, with Beth joining her in pleasing harmony. At Elizabeth's invitation, others soon added their voices, and one bold sailor lad produced amazing melody with a treasured harmonica. The evening ended in an old-fashioned song fest and a decided lifting of spirits, and a request from the Captain that the program be continued each evening.

Next morning Elizabeth was on deck before Beth was up. She was standing at the rail alone, enjoying the gentle, rhythmic motion of the ship and the invigorating Gulf breeze when she sensed that someone was near. He spoke quietly so that she would not be startled.

"Miss Garrett? May I have a word with you?"

"Captain Stuart! Of course, you may! You must be an early riser, too."

"Yes, I enjoy the early mornings at sea. But how did you know it was I?"

"My ears have been well trained to remember voices, Captain."

"Remarkable! I am glad to find you alone. I feel I should apologize for my rather stupid remark last evening regarding your need for light at the piano."

"Please!" she remonstrated. "Let me assure you, I am happiest when people forget that I am blind."

"Remarkable!" he said again. "Then I trust you will forgive a second blunder. I realized when you sang that your voice is exceptionally fine but I didn't know until later, when your friend, Miss Roe, reluctantly disclosed it, that you are a professional musician and entertainer. It was presumptuous of me to assume you would continue for the rest of the voyage. And you should have been properly introduced."

"Please, Captain, I don't *want* that kind of recognition! Just let my music speak for itself! If I can bring a bit of happiness into this troubled world—even for an hour or two—I am greatly rewarded, and I should like very much to continue the entertainment each evening. But just as another passenger who happens to love music! Promise?"

He agreed, thanking her for her generosity.

After that officers and crew vied with each other in providing for the two young westerners who had suddenly become their favorite passengers! Attentive stewards saw that deck chairs and steamer rugs were ready for them when they appeared on deck. At dinner they were invited to sit at the Captain's table, where salty tales of the sea and stories of the great Southwest were exchanged with zest.

Passengers were intrigued by Elizabeth's obvious affection for her native state. "Please don't think that New Mexico is all flat desert," she explained, when opening a program made up entirely of her own songs. "Some people believe it produces nothing but cactus, lizards, and sandstorms! I want you to picture with me its rugged mountains, snow-capped in winter; its deep canyons; the great forests of dark green pine and fir. Then imagine the wide valleys with fertile, irrigated fields; vast herds of cattle and sheep roaming its grasslands; untold mineral wealth—gold, silver, turquoise—all these are to be found in New Mexico. It is a colorful country, with clear air and brilliant sunsets you'd almost have to see to believe!"

They were amazed at her vivid descriptions. "Please tell us how you are so well aware of color," one passenger ventured.

"Of course you would wonder about that!" she said. "You may think it strange, but color does have real meaning for me. Of course, like other intangibles, it must always remain a mystery. For me, color is a combination of impressions. For example, blue is the sky on a cloudless April day; yellow, the warm sunshine; red, the stronger warmth of fire; white, the rich perfume and delicate petals of a certain rose."

They listened with new understanding to her ballads that spoke eloquently of the beauty and romance of her homeland. She closed the program by proudly singing "O Fair New Mexico" and two of her latest works, "The Song of the Flag," and "Our Answer to the Call."

"Thank you for this memorable last evening at sea, Miss Garrett," the Captain said. "We dock tomorrow."

Passengers crowded the decks next morning, eager for the first glimpse of the city's famous sky line.

"It is *fabulous*, Gee-Gee, the buildings are so tall, and so *many* of them—hundreds and hundreds reaching skyward! No wonder they are called skyscrapers. We have never seen a city like this, you may be sure!"

They stood at the rail while the puffing, hooting tug boats slowly nudged the big ship toward the dock. "The air is very clear this morning," Beth went on, "I think we chose the right time to come to New York, everyone says October is the nicest month of the year for weather. Oh, I can see the Statue of Liberty! Holding her torch aloft, just as we have read! But it's so *different* to be here, to actually see it—we must be sure to make a trip out by ferry, so that you can see it better, too."

Elizabeth listened eagerly as Beth described the busy harbor. Other large ships lay at anchor safely distant from each other, while barges and a variety of smaller boats plied the waters around them. She could hear their warning horns sounding, it seemed, in every conceivable key, interspersed with the raucous cry of sea gulls; and finally, her ears caught the slapping sound of the water against the pilings as the ship came to rest at the wharf.

They descended the gangplank in a noisy confusion of sounds, some familiar to Elizabeth, some new. She heard glad cries of greeting as passengers were met by friends or family, and the shouts of stevedores who were unloading cargo below. They joined a slow-moving line to go through customs, and at last, with a porter taking their bags, moved out of the barn-like building to street level. Here the blare of taxicab horns and shouts of news vendors assailed their ears. "Read all about it!" they heard above the din. "U-boat sighted off New Jersey coast!"

"We can be thankful that we are on *terra firma* today!" Elizabeth said fervently.

"The Martha Washington hotel, please," Beth directed the cab driver, and both girls gasped and gripped the seat cushions as the car shot into the traffic and raced madly through the streets.

"I've heard about New York taxi drivers," Elizabeth muttered, "but apparently they are beyond description, too!"

At Mrs. Patterson's suggestion, they had planned to live at the Martha Washington until an apartment suited to their needs and finances could be found. But after the second day, they agreed that the atmosphere of a hotel strictly for women was not to their liking.

"I miss the conversation of a mixed group," Elizabeth said. "A man's way of thinking adds something that seems to be missing when a group of women get together." Beth agreed, thinking of the the stimulating evenings at the Captain's table aboard ship.

"We must do as Dr. Witherspoon advised, and call his friend, Miss Gildner," Elizabeth said. "He wrote that she might help us in locating a place to live."

Laura Gildner was a woman of means, prominent in musical circles, and devoted to the assistance of young musicians newly arrived in the city. She responded to Elizabeth's telephone call with a cordial invitation to tea at her home in Morningside Heights.

"The Witherspoons wrote that you would be coming," she said. "They are very dear friends of mine. I think I can help you in finding a place to live. I do this frequently for Herbert's former students. May I expect you and Miss Roe Sunday afternoon at three?"

They were delighted to accept, and on that October Sunday they quickly learned why Miss Gildner's invitations were so highly prized. Their gracious silver-haired hostess introduced them first to several young musicians who were studying in the city, all of whom had arrived promptly at three o'clock, just ahead of them! Then other guests arrived; among them an aspiring young male pianist, two singers from the Metropolitan, and a teacher of voice from a well-known studio of music, who was presented simply as Madam Parker. The gathering was a happy mixture of youthful ambition and maturity; of talent, with love for music a common bond.

"Will you and Miss Roe stay on for awhile?" their hostess asked when the delightful afternoon was ending. "We must talk further." When the last guest had departed, she came back to the music room, where the girls waited in a high state of anticipation.

"The Witherspoons have spoken of you often, Elizabeth," she said, taking an easy chair near the sofa where they sat. "You know they spend much of their time in New York now."

"And they told me about you, too," Elizabeth said warmly, "and of your many kindnesses to young musicians who come here."

"I am amply rewarded, I can assure you! I consider myself fortunate when I am able to help others, even in a small way.

Now I have something in mind for you."

"An apartment that we could take for the winter?"

"Not exactly, we can find something later, no doubt. But I am thinking of a temporary arrangement that might be agreeable. You see, my home is large, and since I live alone, except for servants, I let a few rooms from time to time to musical friends."

"How wonderful for them!" Elizabeth exclaimed.

"Well," Miss Gildner smiled, "in this way, I am assured of having congenial companions! To get to the point, I have a large double room available for a short time, the month of October to be exact, if you girls are interested. The rent would be minimum, much less than that of a hotel room or apartment. And you may use the kitchen whenever you wish."

"Miss Gildner, you're an angel!" Beth said fervently. "We didn't know where to start looking for a place to live, this city is so tremendous!"

"And now, it actually seems like home!" Elizabeth added. "We can never thank you enough for your kindness."

"Pinch me, Gee-Gee! I must be dreaming!" Beth said the next day as they unpacked their bags in the comfortable guest room. "Three days in New York, and here we are, living in a mansion!"

"Isn't it exciting?" Elizabeth moved about the room, locating chairs, beds and tables with quick hands. "This lovely house, and the stimulating people we meet here. How fortunate for us that Dr. Witherspoon knew Miss Gildner!"

"Yes, isn't she a marvelous person? No wonder musicians like to gather here, she is so genuinely hospitable."

Elizabeth nodded. "I think she is an unusual person, unassuming and kind, not in the least condescending in spite of her wealth. I sensed those qualities in her almost at once. Think of the good she has done through the years! Most young artists are dependent in some way on the help and encouragement of patrons like Miss Gildner. Take my own case, for example. There have been many kind people who have helped me, although I have prided myself on being independent. But it has been like a chain; before Miss Gildner, there was Dr. Witherspoon; and Amy Martin and the girls at the Y. And I would never have met them except for Mrs. Patterson and the fine women of the Woman's Clubs."

"It's really inspiring, when you stop to think about it," Beth mused, "the way events and people are interwoven in a sort of pattern."

"Well, for me it all started with my family who understood my needs, and the wonderful opportunity of attending the Austin school, and the influence of dear Mr. Piner. And again, there is *you*, Beth. I wouldn't be here in New York at all, except for you."

Beth laughed. "Thanks to my wanderlust. But just remember, I wouldn't be here, either, if it were not for *you*. I would never have come alone; you provided the reason for coming, and the courage I lacked as well."

"Who knows, perhaps we were predestined to meet on the train that day years ago!" Elizabeth said. "I was unsure and rather frightened, although I *wanted* to make that trip alone. Mr. Piner and my father said I could do it, and I had confidence in them. Beth, I am constantly reminded that things *do* work out when one has faith! You appeared on that train as though heaven-sent. Then, again, for the San Diego trip, you were free to go with me. And now, you are willing to leave your work at home to share this adventure. I am very grateful to you and to the providence that always seems to care for me."

"Let's hope providence continues to be kind," Beth said half jokingly. "Miss Gildner insists that we take a few days for sight-seeing before we settle down to work. I must confess, this city does sort of overwhelm me. Do you think we'll ever dare ride the subway?"

"I think we'll *have* to, from all we've been told. Yes, we should see the city now, while the weather is good, and as Miss Gildner suggested, leave the museums and galleries for later."

"We can do those on weekends or at off times," Beth agreed. In the days that followed they toured Manhattan Island from Riverside Drive to Battery Park, often traversing Broadway, the fabulous wide avenue bisecting the city from one end of the island to the other. Whenever possible, they sat on the upper level of a sight-seeing bus, but one day rode all the way to Coney Island on the subway. Much to their surprise, they found it a pleasant experience, as they avoided the hazards of rush hour by careful timing.

Central Park was like another world. They took leisurely walks along paths bordered by colorful autumn foliage. They took boat rides on the lakes, visited the Zoo, and ate in quaint little restaurants. They rode in a hansom cab, relaxing to the clop-clop of the horse's hooves on the quiet drive, seemingly far removed from the noise and rush of the great city surrounding them.

An excursion boat took them to Bedloe Island, where the Statue of Liberty stood in lonely splendor, guarding the entrance to the harbor. They walked around the huge, square pedestal, while Beth described the imposing figure looming above.

They took an elevator to an observation platform high inside the shaft, for a panoramic view of the city. "If you wish to go higher, you may take a stairway up to the top of the head," the guide informed them. "One hundred and sixty-eight steps up to another observation platform, the same number on a stairway coming down."

"Shall we?" Beth asked a bit doubtfully.

"Why not? We don't want to miss anything. Besides, the exercise will do us good!"

Later, as they waited for their boat to leave, they paused while Beth read the inscription carved on the base of the statue. Thoughtfully, Elizabeth repeated the closing lines:

"Give me your tired, your poor,
  Your huddled masses yearning to be free,
  The wretched refuse of your teeming shore.
  Send these, the homeless, tempest-tost to me,
  I lift my lamp beside the golden door!"

"Isn't it beautiful, Beth? It makes me so proud to be an American!"

The daily tours were exciting, but exhausting. Returning to their room in the late afternoon, they often fell into their beds to enjoy a brief *siesta*, that welcome custom of the Southwest. Later, refreshed and rested, they were ready for the musical evening which usually followed the dinner hour, when the current proteges of their unusual landlady gathered in the music room.

Other musicians often dropped in, and on one occasion, Madam Parker was present when Elizabeth sang for the group. A few days later, a letter arrived from the Parker studio which Beth read to her incredulous roommate:

"Dear Miss Garrett:

Our mutual friend, Laura Gildner, tells me you will soon be looking for a voice teacher. I have been favorably impressed by the quality of your singing, and should like very much to have a part in the further development of your talent. If you wish to make arrangements for a weekly lesson, there will be no charge. I should consider it a privilege to continue Herbert Witherspoon's tutoring.

Sincerely,
M. Parker"

"How generous she is! But should I accept?" Elizabeth asked

doubtfully.

"How could you refuse? It's a gift from the heart. Don't you see, Gee-Gee, it's just another link in the chain!"

"You're right, I couldn't refuse. Who knows, Beth, maybe I may some day add to the chain, by helping someone!"

"To be of service to our fellow man, to reach out to others, I think it is truly our reason for being," Beth said seriously.

"Dear Beth! Do you realize that you are a splendid example of that philosophy?" Elizabeth said fondly. The words seemed familiar. With a pang of homesickness, she realized Pat had said almost the same thing to *her*, a few months before.

"You *should* be starting your voice lessons soon," Beth said, changing the subject. "After all, further training was a major reason for your coming to New York. I suppose it's time for us both to get busy. We want to do something for the war effort, and we know the Red Cross wants your services after the first of the year, so I should find some kind of work, too. It won't be a bad idea to build our bank acount up a little in the process."

"There are certain friends of mine, not musicians, whom you must meet," Miss Gildner said. "I am thinking of one in particular. She is head of the New York State Commission for the Blind."

"Marian Campbell!" Elizabeth exlaimed, "Oh, how much I have wanted to meet her! I have heard about the fine work the Commission is doing."

"It's as good as done," Miss Gildner said, pleased at Elizabeth's response. "I shall call her at once."

Chapter   11

Suddenly, as if by magic, new links in the chain of Elizabeth's destiny began to appear. The first of these was the propitious meeting with Marian Campbell, head of the State Commission for the Blind.

One of the principal objectives of the Commission was to help the blind adjust to their handicap and achieve social and economic independence whenever possible. Miss Campbell was delighted to learn of Elizabeth's accomplishments, greatly pleased by her spirited determination to pursue new adventures and wider fields of endeavor.

"We face criticism and opposition constantly in our work," Miss Cambell confided. "It is rewarding to find our theories vindi-cated in a career like yours."

Elizabeth, on the other hand, was thrilled to hear of the work being done by the Commission, and by similar groups which were becoming increasingly active in other states.

"How I would enjoy working with the Commission!" she said. "Is there a possibility that I could be useful, when my assignment with the Red Cross is finished?"

"Very definitely," Miss Campbell assured her, "workers are always needed. The program has many facets. Rest assured, we can use you!"

"Then there may be a place for me, too!" Beth said eagerly.

"I am sure there will be. By the way, Miss Gildner tells me you girls are looking for an apartment. It's quite a coincidence, but so am I! In fact, I have found a place I like very much, but it is too large for me alone. I wonder if it might work out for the three of us. We certainly have mutual interests and I have never liked living alone. Why not come tomorrow and look it over?"

It proved to be a most satisfactory arrangement. The apart-ment was adequate and conveniently located. Beth was disturbed, however, by one turn of events. To reach Madam Parker's studio, they walked a few blocks from the apartment down 10th Street to 5th Avenue and boarded a bus which took them to 72nd Street and the location of the studio. After a few of these trips, Elizabeth insisted upon going alone!

"It's simple enough, Beth. Only two streets on 10th to cross, and the traffic policeman and his whistle will help me there. At 5th Avenue, a question or two will assure me I'm getting the right bus. The conductor will tell me when to get off, and there I am, only a few steps from the studio, with no crossing to be made. By reversing the procedure, I can return home alone."

Miss Campbell gave her hearty approval to this, but Beth was apprehensive.

"Don't worry, dear Beth," Elizabeth assured her. "You know I'm always taken care of, somehow. I want so much to do for myself, when I can. *Ten fe*, remember?"

"I know, Gee-Gee, and I want to have faith, as you do! I suppose I'm like a mother hen, too protective, when my chick insists upon leaving the nest."

Marian Campbell laughed. "It is refreshing, Beth, to see your chick doing the things our Commission tries hard to accomplish. One of our aims, as set forth in our charter, is 'to fully encourage each individual to enjoy a normal, active life in his community, according to his ability.'"

"A normal life," Elizabeth repeated. "Yes, it means so much. The hardest part of being blind is being made to feel that one is different. Of course, I know that I must accept certain physical limitations, but I must keep on trying my wings."

With Elizabeth's time more and more occupied with voice lessons and practicing, Beth felt free to take a part-time position with a government agency.

"It's what we both planned to do," Elizabeth said, "you are helping with the war effort and earning something at the same time. I'll be glad when my Red Cross work begins. Much of it will be without pay, though, so I must try to get a few singing engagements. I haven't sent Madrecita any money since we came east and that I must do, after the first of the year. She insists she can manage, but I know her expenses increase as the children grow."

She kept up a lively correspondence with friends in Chicago and El Paso. Both Peggy and Agnes were now married and living out of the city, and Peggy the mother of three-year-old twins!

"Would you believe it, they *both* can carry a tune!" Peggy wrote. "I do more singing now than ever! You should hear us! So you see, your good lessons were not wasted."

"Hurry back to God's country," Mrs. Patterson wrote. "We miss your fine concerts, and we miss you and Beth, always."

Elizabeth wrote regularly to Anne and Madrecita, letters intended for the entire family. How eagerly they listened to the accounts of Gee-Gee's adventures! She told them of a happy reunion with the Witherspoons at Miss Gildner's home, when she and Beth were presented with tickets for the Metropolitan Opera. Dr. Witherspoon would be singing the leading bass role.

Perhaps the most exciting event of all was recorded in one of these letters:

"*Mis queridas*:

"Today I met the renowned Helen Keller! What a fascinating woman! Imagine, if you can, what it would be like, confined to a world of silent darkness as she is, deaf, mute and blind! How remarkably she has overcome these overwhelming obstacles!

"But I must tell you how it happened. Through Miss Cambell, I have met Walter Holmes, editor of the wonderful Zeigler Magazine for the Blind, which is issued in Braille. With a friend, Miss Rhodes, who has known Helen Keller from childhood, he arranged a luncheon, and *these* were the guests:

"Miss Keller and her famous teacher, Mrs. Ann Sullivan Macy; Miss Keller's secretary, Polly Thomson; and my Beth and me. Seven of us, including the hosts, and all with a strong bond of mutual interests. The luncheon was perfectly appointed, with everything designed to put us at ease. Incidentally, Miss Rhodes is blind too.

"I was greatly interested in the method Miss Keller uses to communicate with others. With the finger alphabet, she spells in the palm of her teacher who interprets for her, and who then conveys the ensuing conversation to Miss Keller in the same way!

"She has invited Beth and me to visit her at Forest Hills, her home on Long Island! I am learning the finger alphabet, so that we may communicate directly with each other."

Shortly after that meeting, Miss Keller sent her private car and chauffeur for the two Elizabeths, and they were driven to Forest Hills for a week-end visit.

The house where Miss Keller, her beloved "teacher," and the vivacious young Polly Thomson lived in comfort was spacious and homelike. At their arrival the wide hand-carved door swung open, and Mrs. Macy and Polly appeared to greet them.

"Helen is waiting," Polly said, and led the way to a cheerful room where a wood fire crackled on an open hearth.

Miss Keller sat by the fire, her magnificent German shepherd guide dog at her side. As the dog moved a bit closer, alert to the presence of strangers, she rose, smiling and extending both hands in a gesture of welcome.

Warm greetings were exchanged with Mrs. Macy as interpreter. "Helen is extremely pleased that you are learning the finger alphabet, Elizabeth," she said, "and hopes the two of you can soon dispense with my services. Polly will show you about the house, now, and get you settled in your room before our luncheon is served. We will wait for you here."

"The house is quite large, but simply planned and furnished, so that Helen can get about with little difficulty," Polly explained as they moved from room to room. "You will notice that we have several guest rooms. We have many visitors, and it gives Helen so much pleasure when they stay overnight, or longer, sometimes for days at a time. She loves having company."

Only a brief tour of the grounds was made that day, as the sky was overcast and a few scattered flakes of snow were falling. However, Elizabeth was intrigued by the planning of winding paths through the gardens and natural wooded area surrounding the house. A firm, smooth rope was strung along one side of each path, providing a simple way for Miss Keller to find her way without assistance.

"She loves walking through the grounds with only Sieglinde to accompany her," Polly said, "and especially during the growing season. The gardens are planted advantageously. She loves the scent of roses, lilacs, lilies—so we have a great variety of blossoming shrubs and all kinds of plants, but placed separate from each other so that she can use their fragrance as a guide. Even in winter, the scent of pine and spruce and other evergreens gives her a sense of direction."

How well Elizabeth understood! Sometime I must have a place of my own, she thought, with paths laid out just for me, and my favorite flowers growing, guiding me with their fragrance! And Sieglinde! What a joy it would be to have a faithful guide dog of her own!

Only a few days later, Anne and Madrecita heard all about that unusual week-end.

"And I *sang* for Helen Keller!" the letter concluded. "Let me tell you how she listens. We went to her studio, where she has a very good piano, and through Mrs. Macy, she asked me to sing some of my own compositions.

"I knew then it would always be a pleasure to do anything this gifted woman asked of me, so I responded gladly with O Fair New Mexico and Senorita. She *listened*, first by passing her sensitive finger tips over my throat and lips, as I sang. Then 'teacher' spelled the words for her as I repeated them.

" 'I have never heard such a beautiful voice,' she spelled out in her teacher's hand. Incidentally, they spell very rapidly and communicate with more ease than you can imagine. Her praise embarrassed me a bit! But I asked if I might see her face, and with gentle hands, I saw her noble features. I am sure there could be no lovelier face."

Thus did two unusual women, courageous, determined and talented, *see* and *hear*! A happy relationship was begun, and continually strengthened by mutual respect and understanding in the months that followed, it became a life-long friendship.

The year of 1918 brought an increased tempo of the war in Europe, and shiploads of wounded filled the military hospitals on the eastern seaboard. Elizabeth and Helen Keller, who had also offered her services to the Red Cross, found their appearances greatly in demand. Many of the young patients had suffered loss of sight or hearing, and the visits of these two young women who had risen victoriously above their personal handicaps unfailingly bolstered the morale of the afflicted.

After one of these appearances at a hospital in New Jersey, they were offered an extensive tour of the military base by the commanding officer. Always curious and eager to learn, they accepted.

"Go anywhere you like, ask questions, examine anything you wish," he said, presenting two young aides who would act as their guides. The hours sped by, as accompanied by Mrs. Macy, they examined various kinds of army equipment. They were most fascinated, however, when they climbed into an airplane on display. How amazing it was, with its complicated instruments, fuselage, and great wing spread! It seemed truly a miracle that this great machine could fly through the air! Perhaps some day they would have the experience of riding in one of these fabulous machines!

The tragedy and futility of war preyed on Elizabeth's mind. She spoke of it often to Miss Campbell. "My father, in his way, helped to bring peace to a troubled part of our beloved country," she said. "I often wish I could do something more than I am doing."

"We each have a place in the scheme of things, I firmly believe," Miss Campbell said. "Music brings harmony and peace to many troubled souls. Which reminds me, the warden of Sing Sing Prison has read of your programs and has asked if you would sing for his men. He asks that you present your own compositions."

"How thoughful of him!" Elizabeth was always touched and pleased when asked to sing her own work. "And how rewarding for me, if my music may bring even a little harmony into the disordered lives of those poor men."

Beth continued to accompany Elizabeth on many engagements. A convenient time was chosen for the visit, and the warden sent his car and driver for the two young women. It was a warm, summer day, and a pleasant drive up the Hudson to Ossining, but as they approached the dingy stone walls both girls instinctively felt the gloomy, forbidding atmosphere the prison engendered; a mood intensified for Elizabeth by Beth's description after the car passed through the great iron gates.

"There are so many buildings, Gee-Gee; but they look so bleak and lonely! They are an ugly gray color, although we were told the stone was white originally."

"White, like a tomb!" Elizabeth shivered. "Just think, there are hundreds of unhappy human beings imprisoned here." She felt a strange tie between these unfortunate men and herself.

That afternoon, she poured out her heart to them in song. A few days later, she received an unexpected tribute, a poem written by one of the inmates who heard her sing. The first stanza read:

"Fools, they!
They call her blind!
They call her blind, yet she could lead
A thousand soul-sick men
From cold gray stones and make them heed
The song of wind and rain
From gloomy cell and dewy mead
To sun and stars and sky,
And show the message all could read
Of love and peace and hope.
They call her blind!"

"It is one of the nicest, most understanding compliments ever paid me," she said when Beth read it to her. Later, she translated the entire poem into Braille, and memorized it.

The summer brought happier experiences, too. The family of Marian Campbell owned a sailboat, and often went sailing along the New England coast. At times Miss Campbell invited her young friends to accompany them.

One day when the boat was anchored off the Massachusetts coast, certain members of the group decided to do some deep-sea diving. Knowing their guest to be a good swimmer, they asked her to join them.

Elizabeth loved the water, but this was a new challenge! "Go ahead, Elizabeth," Marian Campbell encouraged her. "If I were younger, and as good at swimming as you, I would try it, too!"

Elizabeth took a deep breath. "What better opportunity could I have? If I ever learn to dive, it's going to be now! With the whole Atlantic Ocean before me, and friends standing by—"

Following the careful coaching of the youthful swimmers, she went overboard as instructed, and came up to enthusiastic cheers. And after the first daring plunge, it was easier.

"It's like singing," she said. "Practice helps!"

Days were largely occupied with Red Cross work. Elizabeth traveled often with Helen Keller for their appearances at army hospitals, and at Miss Keller's invitation, spent much time at Forest Hills. They were deeply saddened by the distressing number of young men who filled the wards, some gravely wounded, many maimed or crippled for life. Their hearts went out to those who had lost their sight.

Putting aside former activities, the two young women put all their energies into the task of bringing cheer and encouragement to these boys, whose lives had been so cruelly changed by war. When the conflict came to a sudden end in November, and a wave of wild rejoicing swept over the country, no one was more deeply thankful than Helen Keller and Elizabeth.

They returned to their former occupations. Miss Keller's life was bound up in continuing work for the blind. Proceeds from publication of two books she had written, added to donations from interested people, made an expanding program possible. Workshops and recreational centers for the blind were being established in more cities, and legislation promoted for the establishment of schools for the blind and deaf.

"When I was a child, only one school would even consider taking a blind deaf-mute," she told Elizabeth. "Without that school, the Perkins Institute, and the patience and understanding of my dear teacher, I would have been committed to an institution, to become a poor, dumb inanimate vegetable. We must have more schools and more trained, dedicated teachers."

The scope of such a program was awesome. Elizabeth's admiration mounted for this indomitable woman, and for her frail, dedicated "teacher," who had devoted her life to Helen and in so doing, had released her charge from the prison of a living death.

Resolving to make the most of her own opportunities, she plunged into work again, resuming lessons with Madam Parker, and preparing for singing engagements.

At the beginning of the winter season, she was presented by the New York press and music publications as "a singer and composer, available for club and church engagements, or interpretative song recitals." Here Madam Parker's quiet influence was an inestimable aid. Elizabeth was deeply grateful; these outlets for her talent and the boost to her declining finances were imperative.

"Can you believe it?" she wrote Anne in the early spring, "I have sung at the Astor and the Brevoort hotels, and recently gave a program for the Federation of Woman's Clubs. And I wrote you that I appeared for the Beaux Arts and the Theater Assembly. Next month, I will sing at the Century Theater, and with several artists on a program at the Pleiades Club. It is so exciting, and marvelous experience."

Reviews by music critics were clipped from papers and magazines and kept Anne and Madrecita informed of Elizabeth's progress.

One which pleased them especially read: "Miss Garrett is known as the songbird of the southwest. She brought to her hearers a message straight from the mountains of her native state in two of her songs, 'Cloudcroft' and 'O Fair New Mexico'. Miss Garrett's voice is pure and clear, with a naturally rich quality . . . her 'Raindrops' and 'Humming Bird' were encores of daintiness and beauty . . ."

The two Elizabeths seized every opportunity to hear the great artists of opera and concert stage. The immortal Caruso was at the height of his career, and to their joy, they were able to attend each opera in which he appeared during their residence in the city. Two years later they were saddened to hear of his failing health, and in a few weeks, of his death in his native Naples. At the age of forty-eight, the glorious voice was stilled.

Another artist whom Elizabeth ardently wished to hear again was Amelita Galli-Curci, the self-taught Italian vocalist who had taken Chicago by storm, appearing for four highly successful seasons with the Chicago Opera.

Shortly after the holidays the papers carried exciting news. Madam Galli-Curci would make her New York debut at the Old Lexington Opera House on January 18, singing the role of "Dinorah."

"We must hear her!" Elizabeth said. But when they hastened to obtain tickets, they found that the house was sold out well in advance. Even the possibility of standing room was uncertain, but on a rainy, cold evening they joined the long line of hopeful standees. Gradually the line moved forward, until only a few persons remained between them and the ticket window. Just then a door slammed, and an attendant shouted: "All space filled! No more room!"

Chilled in body and spirit, they returned home. But marvel of marvels! A few days later, Elizabeth received gift tickets from an anonymous donor for a coming appearance of the incomparable Galli-Curci in beautiful Carnegie Hall!

"It is the most amazing thing, Gee-Gee," Beth said, "that philosophy of yours always seems to bear fruit!"

The New York days continued to bring memorable experiences. "New York votes to ratify the 19th Amendment!" the headlines shouted. At last women would be granted the right to vote! A celebration was in order, and a great rally was scheduled for the Metropolitan Opera House, with Theodore Roosevelt, long friendly to woman's suffrage, as the principal speaker.

How thrilling it would be to see and hear their old friend again! The two Elizabeths arrived very early, in quest of good seats, to find admission was by ticket only! Nonplussed by this unexpected turn of events, they were preparing to leave when a a young man approached, addressing Elizabeth in a commanding decisive voice. "Here are the tickets we have been holding for you. Go right in, Miss Keller!"

Knowing that Helen Keller and her companions were out of the city for an extended stay, Elizabeth hesitated only briefly. Why question such good fortune? "Thank you," she said graciously, and they did as he ordered. After the program they had the pleasure of visiting the former president backstage, reviving pleasant memories of their meeting a few years before in San Diego.

Changes were imminent for Elizabeth and her friends. The office where Beth had been employed was closed. She had no desire to return to the classroom, but was intensely interested in the rapidly expanding field of education and rehabilitation of the blind. She knew that Marian Campbell was leaving to head a Commission in Chicago and had asked Elizabeth to accompany her as her secretary. When Beth was offered a position in Ohio with the State Commission for the Blind, she accepted eagerly.

"It's only a temporary parting, Gee-Gee," she said. "Our paths must always converge."

Helen Keller and Mrs. Macy were traveling extensively, promoting the newly founded American Federation for the Blind, an organization destined to advance the work of former agencies. It was gratifying and thrilling to Beth and Elizabeth to have a part in this great movement.

In Chicago, Elizabeth happily renewed old friendships. She visited the Witherspoon Studios, where she was welcomed royally.

"Are you keeping your voice in training?" Dr. Witherspoon demanded.

"With your help, I certainly shall!" she assured him. The work with the Commission for the Blind was a new challenge, but she knew it must be only temporary. Music was her first love.

Suddenly a new marvel threatened to take the country by storm. Radio! All over the country, people were listening with awkward, inept crystal sets with ear phones to faint and distant music, astonishingly originating as far away as New York and Chicago!

"It is an exciting new field," Elizabeth wrote her family. "Dr. Witherspoon says it may very well revolutionize the field of concert music. If you can find someone with a working set, try to tune in on the 25th. I will be singing on a program just starting, called the Breakfast Club.

"What an exciting age we live in! So many changes and so much yet to come. Oh, I must tell you, Marian and I have gone modern and bobbed our hair! How we agonized over the decision, to bob or not to bob! But now that it's done, I am delighted! It is so easy to care for short hair. I hadn't realized how many precious minutes I spent every day, getting those braids just right."

Again, there were treasured clippings from Chicago papers. A music critic wrote:

"Miss Garrett has a finely trained voice that is essentially Castillian, which means that it is one of the most musical in the world."

Marguerite Silva, star of grand opera, was quoted:

"When I heard Miss Garrett sing her original 'In Sunny New Mexico' I thought it one of the most beautiful things I have ever heard."

The idea of a permanent place of her own was never far from Elizabeth's mind. With the exciting new vistas opening to her, she considered making Chicago her headquarters.

A letter from home brought her to a sudden change of plans. Madrecita needed her desperately. Anne was seriously ill, and there was little hope that she would recover!

As quickly as possible, she cancelled her singing engagements, and asked Miss Campbell to replace her. Next day, she was again aboard the California Limited, the train that had first brought her to Chicago, more than a decade before.

Chapter 12

CHAPTER 12

In the weeks following her sister's death, Elizabeth kept close to her mother's side. Stunned and heartbroken, she found words of consolation empty and meaningless.

Once again, the Garretts sought comfort in the close ties of family. After five years of separation, Elizabeth became reacquainted with her brothers, and with Pauline, who had taken a leave of absence from her secretarial job to help Madrecita with the care of Anne's three motherless children.

Handsome young Pat, home briefly from his travels, tried to divert them with stories of his years in Rome. He would be leaving again soon, this time for South America, where his knowledge of the Spanish language would be useful in his new assignment.

Elizabeth had many questions. She learned that Madrecita had changed least; a becoming sweep of white in Mrs. Garrett's dark hair seemed the only concession to passing years. Poe, though increasingly frail, was still the dependable chef. But Oscar and Jarvis, now tall, deep-voiced young men, had grown almost beyond recognition!

There were visits with old friends, heartwarming, although shadowed by sadness. The Quesenberry family had known their share of sorrow. Bettie's adored little son, Jimmy, had been an early victim of the dreaded influenza epidemic of 1918, and her brother Joseph was mourned as the first United States Army captain to lose his life in the war.

They wept together as they spoke of these loved ones; and of Anne, with her lovely voice and sparkling personality, who had not wanted a career, only a husband and home and children.

"Surely we will see our dear ones again," Mrs. Quesenberry said gently. "There is a poem, that says 'somehow, somewhere'— I can't recall the author."

"I know the poem, I read it often after my father's death," Elizabeth said. "I have it here in a volume of American poets. It's from Whittier's 'Snowbound'."

She rose and took the bulky Braille book from a shelf. Her fingers sought the lines as she read aloud:

> "Yet Love will dream, and Faith will trust,
>   (Since He who knows our need is just),
>   That somewhere, somehow, meet we must."

"I remember the poem," Bettie said as Elizabeth paused. "It is lovely; and it has new meaning for me now."

"I know," Elizabeth said. "Some of the lines seem to have been written for me!" She turned a page and continued.

"I cannot feel that thou art far,
Since near at need the angels are;
And when the sunset gates unbar
Shall I not see thee waiting stand,
And white against the evening star,
The welcome of thy beckoning hand?"

"Oh, Gee-Gee, how I have missed you!" Bettie put her arms about her friend. "Must you go back to Chicago?"

"No, I think not," Elizabeth said slowly. "Although I liked working with Miss Campbell and the American Foundation for the Blind, there are others eager to do that work now. I must settle down to my own vocation, and that can only be music. And I think New Mexico must be my permanent home. At any rate, I'm staying *put* for awhile."

With rigid discipline, she plunged into a strict regime of practice, and after a period of adjustment, began to entertain again.

Engagements in El Paso and other southwestern cities followed. Distances were great, but she made the trips by train alone with little difficulty, except for painful moments of nostalgia, remembering the happy times when Anne had been her companion.

Weeks and months passed, but she was unable to dispell a feeling of empty restlessness. Her concerts no longer provided the challenge of former years. She feared her appearances seemed dull, uninspired.

The family no longer needed her material aid. Madrecita's needs were well taken care of, with her sons educated and working, and Pauline's position as assistant superintendent of schools was secure.

Remembering the advantages and joy of having her own studio, Elizabeth knew she must have a place of her own, where she could get back to composing and teaching with the privacy necessary for serious effort.

She considered possible locations. Las Cruces would be pleasant, with frequent visits with Madrecita, other members of the family, and old friends. But these pleasures in themselves would be distracting.

She thought of El Paso, a convenient location for making recordings, and with the expanding field of radio offering new opportunities. But El Paso was not New Mexico!

Inevitably her thoughts turned to the Pecos Valley, where

she spent her happy early years. Roswell was not a large place, but there was more freedom for her physically in a small town. Its citizens were progressive. She knew of two women's organizations actively engaged in promoting cultural affairs in the growing community. One of these groups had sponsored her concerts there in the past. She was sure her music would be welcome in Roswell.

"There's just one thing, Gee-Gee," Pauline said doubtfully. "I have heard of discrimination there against Spanish-speaking people. Mexicans, they call us, you know."

Elizabeth was silent for a moment. "Yes, I know, although I don't know *why* they feel that way! Could it be that many of the people come from Texas families, and they haven't forgotten the war with Mexico? That doesn't seem reasonable, though. It's the Mexicans who might feel bitter, seems to me."

"I've heard that some Roswellites pride themselves on living in 'a white man's town'," Pauline said frankly.

Elizabeth laughed. "You see, there's an advantage right there, in being blind! Just think, if everyone were blind, the color of one's skin wouldn't matter in the least! No, I won't worry about my Indian blood. My friends soon know I am proud of my ancestry, and the others don't matter."

"You're right of course," Pauline said. "I don't want you to be hurt, that's all. If your mind is made up, let me go with you and help you get settled."

Once the decision was made, they lost no time. A letter to the president of the Roswell Woman's Club asked for assistance in finding an apartment and a possible secretary-companion for Elizabeth. Another letter made a reservation for temporary lodging at Roswell's principal hotel.

"An apartment will do, until I can have a house of my own," Elizabeth said. "I think I have been waiting for just this, Pauline; my own house, in my own home town, in my own New Mexico!"

"Everyone needs roots," Pauline agreed, pleased by her sister's enthusiasm. Elizabeth's apathy since Anne's death had been disturbing. Perhaps this move would provide a needed challenge. One thing was certain, Gee-Gee had the courage to attempt anything!

Although accustomed to traveling alone, Elizabeth was oddly comforted in having Pauline at her side on the bus to Roswell. "Tell me about everything you see," she begged. "I want to renew it all in my mind."

Faithfully, Pauline described the rising *mesas* and foothills as the road climbed toward the Organ Mountain pass, then began its descent into the next wide valley. It was on this road that their father had been so cruelly assassinated; the ranch land formerly held by the Garretts lay only a few miles away.

Below them the great White Sands stretched for many miles to the north, their shimmering, mysterious beauty still hiding the secret of the Fountain murders.

Skirting the sand dunes, the road wound across the Tularosa Basin to the foothills of another mountain range. Here they stopped for lunch in a little Spanish settlement, La Luz.

"I am so glad I could make this trip with you, Gee-Gee," Pauline said as they climbed back into the bus to resume the journey. "My memory needed refreshing, too." With growing interest, she described the changing scenes as the road climbed through rolling hills dotted with sturdy sage-green pinon trees, some gnarled with age, but as Pauline explained, continuing to bear the delicious small pine nut so highly prized by the Indians.

"Isn't it thrilling?" Elizabeth said. "My life began near here, at Eagle Creek; and I shall end my days in my lovely Pecos Valley, where I remember apple blossoms falling like warm, drifting snow! I must sound terribly melodramatic, but today I feel very certain I've made the right decision."

The hotel in Roswell was old, but comfortable. Early next morning, Elizabeth received a telephone call from the president of the Woman's Club. "I would like to send you a visitor," she said. "Mrs. Johnson, who is chairman of the music department of our club, is very eager to talk with you."

An hour later, the sisters were waiting in the lobby when their caller arrived. "Elizabeth!" she said breathlessly. "And Pauline, of course!" She took their extended hands. "Oh, I could hardly wait to see you. Elizabeth, do you remember the Ballard family, who had the farm next to yours when we were children?"

"You can't be Ann Ballard!" Elizabeth said incredulously.

"I am indeed! But now Ann Johnson and a widow, and only recently returned to Roswell to live."

"You were Ida's best friend, I remember well," Elizabeth said. "How envious I was when you and Ida were permitted to ride your own horses to school. I couldn't understand why I couldn't go along."

"What wonderful times we had, playing with Ida and Poe! I must admit, though, you frightened me sometimes, climbing trees and high places right along with the rest of us. You should have seen her, Pauline."

"I've heard so much about those good times on the farm," Pauline said, "I think I missed a lot by being a latecomer in the family."

Another link in the chain, Elizabeth thought, as they found comfortable chairs and settled down to talk. "Do you know, Ann, it was in your home that I first heard a piano played? I still remember the thrill it gave me."

"Mother treasured that piano," Ann Johnson said, "and I am grateful that she instilled the love for music in me. It means so much to me now, to be a part of the musical community here."

"Isn't it a coincidence," Ann agreed. "Elizabeth—or should I say Gee-Gee? I see you have a new name; it was 'Lisbet' when I first knew you! I came to ask you to share my home, at least for awhile."

"How kind of you!" Elizabeth said, then hesitated. "But are you sure I should? I must warn you, my habits are rather unorthodox at times. For example, you might find my practice periods annoying—"

"I considered that before I came. I'm sure we can work out an agreeable schedule. I practice too, so we'll be even on that score! I am out of the house a good part of each day, however, with other interests. My work with the Woman's Club takes much of my time. You could use my piano, too, if you will be giving piano lessons."

"It would be wonderful for me!" Elizabeth said. "If you are sure you'd like to try me, I'll engage a part-time companion before Pauline goes home, and then I promise I will be quite independent."

"I may know someone who would fit right in," Ann said, "a girl who lives with her parents on my street. She is just out of school, and hopes to do secretarial work eventually, but she loves to sing and has a very good voice. I think she would count it a real privilege to work with you."

"Well!" Pauline laughed. "I think I can go home any time. I can see that you will be looked after very well, Gee-Gee. And I almost forgot to tell you—before that darling May Rees left for her new teaching job in Las Vegas, she showed me a stack of notes and memos she had made of stories you told her about your childhood and school years, and of Papa's guidance and patience. She says a book should be written telling these things and revealing the Pat Garrett no one except his family really knew."

"I would like that very much," Elizabeth said simply.

Chapter 13

CHAPTER 13

Charlotte St. John was the typical "girl next door," vivacious and energetic, and youthfully awed by her association with the talented Miss Garrett, who immediately found her services invaluable.

Charlotte's most important duty was reading the daily mail and newspapers to Elizabeth. How thrilling she found the letters from famous people all over the world! Elizabeth took keen delight in her correspondence with friends, and letters from Beth, Marian Campbell, the Witherspoons, Editor Walter Holmes and a score of others kept her well informed of what they were doing, thinking and planning, and she responded promptly with news of her own. Her treasured typewriter gave her the satisfaction of answering without assistance.

There were frequent letters from Helen Keller and Mrs. Macy, which always closed with the phrase: "Sieglinde sends a lick and a wag." "That wonderful Sieglinde!" Elizabeth often said. "When I have my own place, I *must* have a dog!"

In one mail there came a beautifully posed photograph of Helen, with a message inscribed in her own inimitable block style: "Elizabeth dear, you are like the arm of faith defying darkness. Strong and beautiful, you are pictured in my heart forever."

With loving hands, Elizabeth held the photograph as Charlotte described it in faithful detail.

Pleased by the warm welcome she received in Roswell, Elizabeth became a member of the Woman's Club and the Business and Professional Women's Club. Always grateful for the encouragement she had received from such organizations, she freely offered them her time and talent. Life seemed meaningful again, as she plunged into the pursuits she had chosen: teaching, composing, entertaining and community work.

In an atmosphere reminiscent of Laura Gildner's music salon in New York, Ann Johnson's living room became a meeting place for musicians of both sexes who were eager to know Elizabeth.

She was often asked to direct group singing. To her great delight, she discovered several fine voices among the women. Other impromptu musicals were enhanced by the addition of a talented Mexican-American violinist and two excellent amateur pianists, one a business man, the other a teacher of English at the Roswell Military Institute.

"Isn't it a joy, to find all this talent in our small community?" Elizabeth said after a musical evening. "I've been thinking; why can't we have a singing group here, something like the Octette at the Austin school?"

"Why not?" Ann agreed. "How would we begin?"

"We should have at least six voices, yes, six would be right I think. Two first and two second sopranos—"

"Ruth Martens! Helen Goodsell, Aileen Smith, Harriet Robertson—"

"Four splendid voices right there!" Elizabeth said happily. "And two altos, you for one. And Amelia Tigner!"

"But you should be included," Ann protested.

"I'll direct. And I can always fill in, if needed. We should have other substitutes, too, for emergencies or to fill vacancies if they arise. Charlotte should be one understudy, her voice is improving by the day since she is practicing regularly. And there's Inez Boyle, and others. And we should have an accompanist."

"Caroline Morehead?"

"Of course! And Lee Henrichs or Colonel Troutman would substitute if needed, I'm sure. Now if they will all accept! It would mean regular practice and some sacrifice of time. Trips out of town, too, if we are asked to sing elsewhere."

"They'll accept," Ann said confidently. "Those girls love to sing.'

Ann was right. The singing group, launched at an enthusiastic meeting in her living room, was a success from the start. Suddenly there were more requests for appearances of the Elizabeth Garrett Sextette than they could fill!

"You are receiving excellent press coverage," Charlotte said as she read the newspapers one morning. "The Daily Record is giving you glowing reviews."

"Although I am virtually a newcomer!"

"To Roswell, maybe, but not to the state. I think the writer knows more about you than you realize."

"I should thank him, or her. Find out who he is!"

"Oh, I know the writer," Charlotte said. "His name is Will Robinson. He is quite well known as a newsman, his columns are carried in papers all over the state."

"Will Robinson? Why, that was the name of a young man who once saved my life! He pulled me out of the big irrigation canal in Las Cruces. I remember it well, although I was only three years old. He was a young newspaper reporter. Charlotte, it must be the same person. We must get in touch with him."

"I have followed your career with great interest, Elizabeth," the veteran newsman said, when he and his wife came to call a few days later. "Just as I once followed your father's."

"You knew my father!"

"Oh, yes, I knew him well. In fact my editorials in the Las Cruces papers, supporting him and openly criticizing the corrupt politicians opposing him—well, these columns made me so many enemies that life in Las Cruces became unbearable! I came to Roswell about the time your father left Las Cruces to live in El Paso. But I have kept up with the Garretts, and especially with the family songbird."

"How fortunate for me that our paths have crossed," Elizabeth said, "not only that first eventful time, but now when my career needs the support of your paper. Will Robinson, you are truly a friend in need!"

Helen Keller was author of several books during her lifetime; books which were widely read and created much interest in the possibilities of education for the blind and the blind-deaf. The third of these, "Midstream," was published about the time of Elizabeth's move to Roswell. A few weeks later she received a copy in the mail.

"The book is dedicated to Mrs. Macy, Helen Keller's teacher," Charlotte said, "but listen to the inscription to *you* on the same page: 'To our dear Elizabeth. There is a flavor about her friendship that leaves the heart hungry for a touch of her hand and the sound of her lovely voice. She lives to bring light, happiness, and music to all.'"

Elizabeth's eyes filled. "How beautifully she expresses her thoughts! She is a dear person, Charlotte."

"She is, indeed!" Charlotte thumbed through the index eagerly. "Oh, in the middle of the book, there is more about you! One, two, *three* or more pages devoted to you! They begin like this:

'A comrade in the dark, who lives far away now, but used to visit me often is Elizabeth Garrett. When books began to appear about the thrilling adventures of Elizabeth's father, Pat Garrett, the famous sheriff of New Mexico, and the hair-breadth escapes of Billy the Kid, I felt as one might if somebody took liberties with his family. For Elizabeth has told me so much about her father and the Kid that they seem to belong to me, somehow.*

Charlotte stopped in wonderment. "What a remarkable per-

*From "Midstream" by Helen Keller, published by Doubleday and Company, 1929.

son! Totally deaf, unable to see, and yet so understanding, so perceptive. Do you suppose I can meet her some day?"

"Why not?" Elizabeth said. "I must see her again, too. There are many things we must do, Charlotte. Let's put that high on our list! In the meantime, how I shall enjoy your reading this book to me! And will you *please* call me Gee-Gee? Miss Garrett is a bit too formal for me."

"I must have a house of my own, as soon as I can manage it," Elizabeth said often, "a place with more privacy. I can't inflict practicing and composing at all hours on Ann and my neighbors, since I seem to do my best work when others are sleeping."

She recalled slipping out in the early morning hours to her little studio in El Paso, using great care to return to Mrs. Patterson's before the family was up!

The limitations of her earnings made the dream dismally remote. But interested friends and other civic-minded Roswell residents, knowing of these circumstances, took matters into their own hands. They asked her permission to arrange for the building. Some of the planning and actual labor would be donated.

At first, she refused their offer. "I cannot accept charity," she informed her devoted Charlotte.

"The sincere desire of friends to do something helpful for you is not that *kind* of charity," Charlotte remonstrated. "It is love!"

"Helen Keller once told me of a similar decision she had to make," Elizabeth said thoughtfully. "Many prominent people took an interest in the work she was doing for the blind and deaf-blind. But she was too proud to accept personal financial help. At one time, Andrew Carnegie asked her to accept a lifetime income from him and Mrs. Carnegie, to assist her in carrying on her work. She refused. But a few years later, when her beloved teacher was failing in health, and employment of an additional companion was a necessity for them both, she realized her pride was a selfish stumbling block, preventing her caring for Mrs. Macy properly and continuing the work they loved. Mr. Carnegie had assured her the offer was always open, and she humbly wrote and accepted."

"How sensible of her! And kind, too, really, to allow him the privilege of helping."

"You are right, Charlotte. One should never refuse a gift of love."

"Then we'll tell our good friends you accept their generous offer!" Charlotte said happily.

"Lee Henrichs, of course. He is behind all this, you know. He is not only a wonderfully kind person, but a good business man from all I hear. I think we might compromise a bit. He can arrange the financing of the house and lot, and I will pay a nominal rent, with the privilege of outright purchase at a later time, if I can afford it."

"This house must be built exactly as you want it," the architect said at their first meeting. "Please tell me what you have in mind."

"First, I would like it built of *adobe* brick," she said, "that is, if it would be practical."

"*Adobe* is well suited to this dry climate," he agreed.

"Good! I've thought about my house for a long time," she said happily. "It should be set well back from the street, so my early morning practice won't annoy anyone. And no steps anywhere, please; slightly inclined ramps and hand rails are very useful for me. And will you plaster the house with white stucco, and let the window trim be blue, my little mother's favorite color."

The architect followed her plans with care, offering many helpful suggestions as the blueprint was made. "It is perfect!" she declared joyously when he described the final draft. "When I move into this house, I hope I never have to move again!"

Elizabeth kept busy as she waited for the completion of the house. Days were full, with music pupils, rehearsing with the Sextette, or attending club meetings with Ann Johnson and other friends. Charlotte went about her own affairs, except for the period of each day so important to them both, when the mail and daily papers were read and correspondence answered.

Charlotte had completed a secretarial course and planned to do office work after Elizabeth was settled in her own house. "But please, Gee-Gee," she said, "let me continue to help with your mail. It's just too interesting to give up!"

In November, their routine was interrupted by a trip to Albuquerque, where John Philip Sousa and his band of one hundred musicians presented a program at the University of New Mexico. Guests of honor on that occasion were the governor of the state and Miss Elizabeth Garrett.

Elizabeth had met the famed conductor at the Witherspoon Studio in Chicago several years before. She was surprised that he recalled the meeting. During the course of the program, he made an announcement:

"The next number is the premiere of my 'New Mexico March'," he said. "In it, I have incorporated strains of your state song, along with Indian strains and Spanish folk songs. We salute your Governor, your state and Miss Garrett, composer of 'O Fair New Mexico'."

One day's mail brought news of two appointments of note. The General Federation of Woman's Clubs had made Elizabeth Chairman of Folk Music in the Department of Fine Arts, a position of national scope. And the Governor asked her to serve on the Board of Regents of the New Mexico School for the Blind.

"Of course I know without asking that you'll accept," Charlotte said. "I've been thinking, Gee-Gee; if you were only *paid* for all the things you do, you could soon afford that dog you want so much."

Elizabeth sighed. "You're right. The Folk Music appointment, especially will involve a great deal of correspondence and will be time consuming. I only regret, though, that I can't do more! I want to help with the fine work The Woman's Clubs are doing; I can't forget what they did for me. And it is so gratifying that our state now has a school for the blind! No one knows better than I just what that means to blind children, or those visually handicapped. No, I don't want to be paid for such service."

"But you do so much! The trips you make, for instance, to sing for the club meetings all over the country! They only pay your expenses, and meanwhile, you are away from your music pupils."

Elizabeth laughed. "You know I love those trips, Charlotte!"

"But right here in this community, you give so much of your time," Charlotte persisted. "And I know you seldom receive a fee for your concerts, and nothing for all the lovely performances by the Sextette—"

Dear Charlotte, Elizabeth thought, so young and yet so practical!

"When I came to Roswell I made a rather difficult choice," she explained. "Opportunities for earning were greater in the city. Chicago, for instance. I could have taught in a school of music, and there were frequent calls for entertainment in restaurants or private clubs. But living in a small town gives me freedom I could never have in a city. It means so much to be able to walk from one part of my town to another, to have neighbors who are permanent, to be a part of a community. I only ask that I can earn enough to take care of my material needs."

Charlotte shrugged. "Well, here's another letter that looks interesting, and you'll like it, because it means another trip. Governor Dillon asks you to be his guest and a member of his party on Governor's Day next month at the Carlsbad National Caverns."

Elizabeth's face glowed with pleasure. "Oh, good! I have wanted so much to visit those great caverns!"

"And you should!" Charlotte said. "Our senior class went

there, two years ago. It is a subterranean wonderland, really! I could hardly believe my eyes."

Carlsbad, a hundred miles to the south, was a small town very much like Roswell until the opening of the tremendous caverns nearby brought national attention and many visitors to the community. Old timers talked of mysterious unexplored caves, but it was only since the turn of the century that their true magnitude had become known. Now a part of the National Park system, the trails leading down into a number of great underground chambers were safely negotiated every day by hundreds of tourists. The entire explored area was adequately lighted by electricity.

Elizabeth listened in awe as the park ranger accompanying their party described the largest of these chambers, which they had reached after a lengthy descent through narrow passageways. She immediately felt the vastness of the great cavern as they entered, sensing that the low ceiling of the passageway was suddenly gone. Sounds of voices and footsteps told her that an immense empty space surrounded them.

"This one room is more than a half mile in length, and 400 feet wide," the ranger explained. "It is filled with an amazing variety of stalactites and stalagmites which have been many thousands of years in the making."

Their guide took a special interest in explaining many details to Elizabeth and insisted that she touch some of the delicate formations, although visitors as a rule were admonished not to do so. "They are as different as petals of flowers," she said, "and when I tap them, I can detect a faint musical tone!"

They paused on one trail by a still, unfathomed pool of water. "This is called the Wishing Well," the ranger said. "Some say the wish you make here is sure to come true." I wish that I might write a song about this marvelous work of nature, Elizabeth thought.**

In another of the vast rooms of the cavern, they paused again while the guide described the mightiest stalagmite of all.

"We call this great formation the Rock of Ages," he said. "It is estimated that sixty-five million years have passed since its beginning. We regret that our Ranger Quartette isn't with us today. Usually we have a rather impressive little ceremony, when all lights are turned off and the rangers sing the hymn that gave the Rock its name."

"Perhaps Miss Garrett would sing for us," the Governor

**"When We Walk the Cavern Trails Together" was one of the fifty or more songs published in later years by Elizabeth Garrett.

suggested.

Elizabeth agreed readily. She knew the hymn well, from the days when she had directed the choir in El Paso. Gradually the lights were dimmed until completely extinguished, and the crowd was enveloped in a total darkness that possibly no one other than the singer had ever experienced. There was a moment of awesome silence, then the pure soprano voice poured forth in the notes of the lovely old hymn. It was an unforgettable experience for singer and listeners.

Disturbing news awaited Elizabeth upon her return from Carlsbad. Poe was seriously ill; her mother needed her. With Charlotte's help, she prepared for another journey and was soon on a bus bound for Las Cruces.

Once again the Garrett family drew close in sorrow, as Poe slipped away. Although deeply saddened by his death, they found solace in the knowledge that the valiant, twisted body now rested in peace.

The many unexpected tributes and honors bestowed upon her filled Elizabeth's heart with gratitude. How satisfying to feel secure and loved in the community that would always have her loyal devotion. And now the house was finished! She hastened to write Pauline and Madrecita:

"At last it is accomplished, and I am settled in *La Casita*. My little house and I are eagerly awaiting your visit. I have so much to show you! Friends have been more than thoughtful, their house-warming gifts have made my house a home! The alcove off my studio is filled with lovely houseplants, many in bloom. The studio is filled with treasures. And the kitchen! For the first time, I can try my hand at cooking, something I have always wanted to do. You should see the clever pots and pans showered on me!

"But the most wonderful gift of all arrived the day I moved in, a beautiful Steinway grand piano! A letter came with it, explaining that it was paid for by donations from the school children of the state, to thank me for their song, O Fair New Mexico! I am deeply touched, and still numb with surprise.

"Lee Henrichs has admitted that a few generous friends helped the children out a bit. But I am not to know who they are, although I have my own ideas. How wonderfully kind people are!"

The very next week, Mrs. Garrett and Pauline came up the walk to *La Casita*. The front lawn was newly planted with grass, and shaded by a venerable elm tree the builders had spared.

Her expressive face alight, Elizabeth stood at the open blue-painted front door with arms outstretched. "Come in, *queridas!* Welcome to *La Casita!*" She embraced them warmly. "I am so glad you are finally here."

They entered a large studio-living room, with twelve foot white-washed walls and viga-supported ceiling. A picture window revealed a landscaped area at the rear of the house. The east wall of the room included a sunny alcove with a comfortable window seat and a profusion of flowering plants, the west wall was dominated by the piano.

"Such a beautiful room!" Pauline exclaimed. "A perfect setting, Gee-Gee, for you and your Steinway. How fitting that it came from the school children. I am sure you have sung at assemblies in every school in the state, and many times for some."

"I *wondered* why you objected to having my piano sent to me," Elizabeth said. "It was too old and battered, you said; I should replace it, although I knew I couldn't afford a new one! Now I realize that you were in on the conspiracy. The Las Cruces children were among the most generous contributors!"

"But *I* didn't know," Madrecita said. "I suppose they thought I was not to be trusted." She looked about with pleasure. Colorful Indian rugs, native pottery, and handwoven wall hangings displayed the influence of Spanish and Indian cultures. The Steinway dominated the room, but Madrecita was drawn to the round bee-hive shaped corner fireplace, which was flanked by accessories of Old Mexican design.

Two portraits hung on one wall, an excellent likeness of Madrecita, and the autographed photograph of Helen Keller.

"You see, you are in distinguished company, Madrecita," Pauline said. "And with just the proper setting for two lovely ladies."

"*Muy bonita*," Mrs. Garrett smiled, "it is a very pretty room."

"Next you must see my kitchen," Elizabeth said. "I adore it; it has every convenience for me." Mrs. Garrett examined each detail with great interest, the gas range, an electric refrigerator, and easily accessible cupboards and drawers. Table and chairs made by Old Mexico artisans added a unique accent.

"The gas stove," Madrecita said anxiously, "is it safe for you?"

"It is safe, dear Mama, although you may be sure I am at all times very careful. Let me show you. The oven control is simple, one turn for low heat, the next for medium, another for high, and reverse turn for broil. And for the top burners, there's an automatic pilot light. When I turn the gas on, it lights at once. I know, because I hear a little pop! I simply hold my hand above the burner, like this, to determine the heat needed as I turn the control."

Elizabeth moved with assurance through the rest of the house. Two bedrooms, each with twin beds, opened from a hall which was spacious enough to accommodate wide shelves for bulky Braille magazines and books. There were roomy clothes closets, and a bathroom where a cabinet top held an assortment of bottles of perfume, lotions and facial cream. "Ah, Gee-Gee," Pauline smiled, recognizing these sweet-smelling indulgences, "I see your habits haven't changed."

The patio was inspected last, a large grassed area enclosed by six-foot plastered walls that insured shelter and privacy. An antique brass bell hung above a blue-painted gate. A fireplace designed for outdoor cooking was built into one wall. Rose bushes and shrubs and two young apple trees were planted at suitable spots, but Pauline noticed one sturdy sapling which she could not identify.

"I had to have a pecan tree," Elizabeth explained, "like the one at the Austin school. That tree was my greatest comfort when I was homesick and lonely. It had a real part in my education!"

That evening, with Charlotte and Ann in attendance, Elizabeth broiled steaks for her visitors on the outdoor fireplace grill. A pot of *frijoles* cooked according to Poe's incomparable recipe was an accompanying dish.

When their visit ended a few days later, Mrs. Garrett and Pauline returned to Las Cruces with the comforting knowledge that Elizabeth was secure and happy in her own home.

Chapter 14

CHAPTER 14

The American Foundation for the Blind was steadily becoming a driving force in the east. Marian Campbell, whose life was dedicated to the cause, kept Elizabeth informed of the progress being made. She reported that legislation promoted by the AFB had brought about passage of a section of the Social Security Act providing relief for needy blind persons. Laws had also been passed granting funds for free Braille books.

Their goal, however, was not only public relief for the needy blind, but restoration to social and economic independence whenever possible. To this end, specially trained workers were engaged in teaching the blind to adjust. Scholarships were provided for those preparing for a special vocation.

The AFB steadily pushed the establishment of needed agencies, more recreational centers, and Braille libraries. They promoted the manufacture of Braille timepieces and games. Helen Keller was a permanent member of the staff. Her personal appearances throughout the country were not highly successful in fund raising, but invaluable in educating the public by demonstrating that the blind may live useful, dignified lives.

Elizabeth was thrilled to hear of the progress being made. How different from the time of her birth, when the blind were often considered only a burden to society!

The most exciting news from the east, however, told of a unique school that had been established in Morristown, New Jersey.

While guide dogs had always been used in a limited manner by certain blind individuals, suitable dogs were obtained only by chance. When World War I left many blinded veterans, the German government established schools for the special training of guide dogs for these men. The success of the experiment was electrifying.

As a result, an agency known as The Seeing Eye had come into being, devoted solely to the training of dogs for blind persons in the United States.

"I know you have wanted a guide dog for some time," Marian Campbell wrote. "Please consider the Seeing Eye. We have been told that only a small percentage of the blind can use these highly trained dogs. The recipient must be in good health, strong, active, able to walk at a brisk pace, and between the ages of fifteen and fifty-five years. They are not for the timid. But recalling the girl who so eagerly tried deep-sea diving, I am confident you can qualify."

A specially trained dog of her own! A trusted companion, day and night, granting her priceless freedom and independence! Could it possible?

"We must get all the information, Charlotte," she said. "We will write Morristown this very minute and find out what one does to get one of these wonderful dogs."

What an alluring dream! Deflated all too soon, however, as the desired information came back to them. Although the Seeing Eye Institute was a non-profit organization and generously endowed, a great deal of expense was involved in the breeding, care, and meticulous training of these special dogs and a sizeable fee was required. The prospective buyer must live at the school for a period of several weeks, while dog and owner became adjusted to each other.

The trip east and back would be expensive. And Elizabeth would be away from her music pupils for an extended period, with the loss of income their lessons provided.

"Your point has been proved, Charlotte," Elizabeth said ruefully. "I should earn more money. Even if I work harder and try to be very frugal, it would take years to save enough for this undertaking. I'd better forget the Seeing Eye, and find a good little dog as a companion."

"It isn't like you to give up so easily," Charlotte protested. "What happened to your old motto? *Ten fe*, Gee-Gee!"

Elizabeth laughed. "I do sound pessimistic, don't I! I'm afraid I *am* a bit discouraged. But who knows? Something may work out yet! I'll hang on to my dream a little longer. Thanks, Charlotte, for reminding me."

Life settled down to an even tenor. The regularly scheduled music pupils came and went, and early evening hours brought many pleasant interruptions and diversions. The patio became the accepted place for meetings and social gatherings of the Sextette and other friends during the fine weather Roswell usually enjoyed. Rehearsals and musical evenings logically centered about the Steinway in the roomy studio.

Elizabeth's love for animals and birds had endured since childhood, but her mode of living had ruled out owning any kind of pet, and especially a guide dog, which she so desperately longed to have. Now, with the privacy provided by her new home, she could change this state of affairs. A gray and white cat, called Smut because of his sooty face, was the first addition to the household, a lovable vagabond who roamed house and yard at will.

Jerico, a canary soon known as Jerry, was installed next in the alcove, his cage hung in the midst of the greenery.

"Isn't it miraculous that so much music can come from that little throat?" Charlotte said in surprise.

"Yes, he's just a tiny feathered bundle of melody! The calls and whistling of birds have always fascinated me, and especially the warbling of song birds, but a canary's singing is simply incredible! Have you noticed that Jerry starts singing after he hears piano music? I am sure he will soon be singing right along with me. Now when I get a dog, my family will be complete."

In the privacy of her own house, Elizabeth was able to turn again to composing, working mostly at night when she was free from interruptions. The still, quiet hours when most of the world was sleeping brought inspiration that eluded her by day.

When Charlotte had returned to her parents' home for the night and other visitors had left, Elizabeth set to work on her most ambitious undertaking, an Easter Cantata which she based on the twenty-third Psalm and other Biblical passages.

During the Lenten season the Sextette, with Lee Henrichs at the piano and Elizabeth directing, presented the lengthy work entitled "Servant, Master and Lord" in several neighboring cities.

There were tears of joy and humble gratitude in *La Casita* when Charlotte read the favorable reviews from Roswell and El Paso papers. "But one thing bothers me," Charlotte said. "This splendid work isn't bringing you in one solitary cent!"

Elizabeth laughed. "It wasn't written for money, that may be the reason."

"You should copyright everything you've done!" Charlotte insisted. "So far, only a few numbers you had published in Chicago are under copyright."

Elizabeth sighed. "You're right. I must take care of it soon." But Charlotte shrugged in resignation. Soon might be a long time with Gee-Gee, when it came to money matters!

Elizabeth respected Charlotte's judgment, however, and resolved to act on her suggestions. How she had come to depend upon this sensible young girl!

"My parents are moving away soon," Charlotte interrupted her thoughts, "to live in Albuquerque. They think I should go with them, but I don't want to give up my good position at the Military School, and I can't bear the thought of missing your daily mail! So I will simply find another place to live."

"Why not *La Casita*?" Elizabeth spoke without hesitation. "We do get along beautifully, Charlotte, and there's plenty of room for us both. Now that the cantata is finished, I promise to stop my night sessions so you can get your sleep."

"Oh, Gee-Gee, I would love it! You needn't worry about disturbing me at night, I sleep like a log! And frankly, I have never liked your living entirely alone."

"Good! Then it's settled. It will be a fine arrangement, I know! But don't forget, you're not to usurp my privilege of preparing lunch for us every day as I have been doing!"

"I wouldn't think of it," Charlotte laughed, "I don't like to cook that well." She paused. "Oh, I have the greatest idea! Say no if you wish, I won't mind. But you know I would expect to pay for my room as I would in any other home. Would you allow me to buy an interest in the house?"

"Why not!" Elizabeth said. "We can simply divide the payments, and *La Casita* will be *our* house! When you marry—as you are sure to do—I will buy your interest. I can tell you now, I have never liked being alone at night. Fate was good to me when you entered my life, Charlotte."

That year was, indeed, a fateful one. Elizabeth was incredulous when the word came that the Business and Professional Women of New Mexico wished to underwrite a Seeing Eye dog for Miss Elizabeth Garrett! They would not only furnish the Seeing Eye, but would also pay the expenses of the trip to Morristown and back.

Again, she was stunned and humbled by the generosity of her fellow man. But she had learned to accept the gifts of love.

"You must go with me, Charlotte. We'll take an extra day and visit Helen Keller."

"How I would love it!" Charlotte's eyes sparkled with excitement. "Let's get busy, we have a lot of letters to write."

The trip was made by bus, so that they might see the country en route, stopping briefly for visits with former Roswell friends in Ohio and Pennsylvania. New York was next, where they stopped for a few days of visiting with friends for Elizabeth, and sightseeing for Charlotte.

Elizabeth Roe, now married and living in Florida, had urged them to visit her in her new home, but their limited time and budget forced them to decline her invitation. "Surely we will meet again, dear Beth," Elizabeth wrote. "You must see your many El Paso friends, and visit me in *La Casita*."

A delightful culmination of their holiday was luncheon at Forest Hills with Helen Keller, Polly Thomson, and Ann Sullivan Macy. Mrs. Macy's unflagging courage in spite of failing health and near blindness inspired all who knew her. How fitting that Helen, who had been liberated from silent darkness by the patient understanding of this unselfish woman, would care for her so tenderly now in her time of need!

After Charlotte saw her friend settled in the large, two-storied house of the institute at Morristown, she took a homeward bound train, leaving Elizabeth to the serious business of qualifying for a Seeing Eye dog.

The first assignment had nothing to do with dogs. She was requested to orient herself thoroughly with the house where she and several other trainees lived. From long experience, she accomplished this with comparative ease, and in a few days, when she had become familiar with the grounds, she was allowed to take a trial test with a dog in the grassy, tree-filled yard.

Typewriters were available, and Charlotte received daily accounts of her progress.

"I started out bravely with a huge German police," she wrote. "His ideas of guidance were ecstatic notions of pulling and hauling anyone for whom he was responsible, which he did with irrepressible vigor! After taking many a tumble, I wondered if I could be rid of this happy extrovert before my bruises became too numerous. I asked if I might work with a smaller and more lady-like dog. I was then assigned a highly intelligent, pleasant dispositioned German shepherd who had real ideas of guiding, not pulling. She is called Teene, and already we have developed a remarkable understanding companionship. Teene is my dog!"

Although the trainers frankly admitted they preferred candidates who were still in their teens, they were satisfied with the progress Elizabeth made. She had passed her tests, but it remained to be seen whether Teene accepted her without reservation.

"In the last phase of training," she wrote, "I sat alone in a room, arms dropped loosely at my sides, wholly at ease. A ball of fresh meat was in my left hand. A trained observer was in a position where he could study Teene's reactions, but she was not aware of his presence. Teene came into the room. She explored it carefully, then came confidently to my side and took the meat ball from my hand. For me, it was a joyful moment. By that act, Teene accepted me as being worthy of her affectionate, vigilant care and protection."

Teene made the trip to Roswell by special crate in the baggage car, an ordeal which offended her sense of dignity. It was soon forgotten, however, in the happy reunion with her new owner and the adventure of exploring her new home.

The homecoming was a momentous occasion. For Teene, it meant permanence and an adoring mistress; for Elizabeth, a loyal companion and greater freedom than she had ever known.

At first, Smut displayed his open resentment to the intruder, but a sort of unstable truce was arranged. Teene was assigned her own private domain, the patio, which Smut entered at his own risk. Teene was patiently trained to avoid Smut's corner of the kitchen. Meanwhile, Jerry surveyed all these adjustments with a curious eye. It soon became obvious, however, that a real affection was growing between the dog and the feathered singer. When Jerry unpredictably burst forth with his inimitable trills, Teene sat eyeing his cage in amazed approval, after which Jerry cocked his head to one side and looked at Teene with a kind of "what do you think of that" expression, much to the amusement of Elizabeth and Charlotte.

Roswellites soon grew accustomed to seeing Elizabeth and Teene on the way to the grocery store, the library, a picture show, or Sunday morning church service. Brisk exercise was a part of their daily schedule, and often they walked for that reason alone. Although friends felt pangs of denial when they were seldom called to accompany her as in former times, they soon shared her pride in her greater independence.

In spite of Elizabeth's confidence in Teene's guidance, Charlotte entertained disquieting thoughts concerning her safety.

"I just can't understand it, Gee-Gee. How can you depend on a dumb animal to take you where you want to go?"

"Dumb, but very intelligent, you must remember. Of course, I must guide Teene, to some extent. I must know how many blocks to my destination, and the direction. So many blocks to the right, so many to the left—I must count with care. It is Teene's responsibility to see that I get there safely. We work together."

Later that day, Charlotte witnessed a scene that allayed her fears. Unknown to Elizabeth, she watched as Teene led her mistress briskly down the walk toward a shopping center. In the middle of the block, Teene began slowing her pace, and finally sat down in front of Elizabeth, completely blocking her way. Puzzled, Elizabeth felt cautiously to each side and above her, finding no obstacle. Then reaching down to explore the walk, she discovered a garden hose stretched across the walk and elevated slightly in the air! The hurdle was cleared, and dog and mistress continued without hesitation.

Teene's loyal devotion to her mistress was obvious. At home, harness removed, she was a relaxed, lovable pet, reveling in the attentions she received. She liked especially the grooming sessions when Elizabeth brushed her thick, dark coat until every hair was in shining order.

As she worked, Elizabeth talked to Teene. "We always have to look our best, you dear," she said. And Teene's telegraphic tail tapped out complete agreement.

At the given signal, however, a rattle of her harness, Teene was instantly alert and all business, ready for her appointed work.

Elizabeth was accompanied by her dog on all trips about the state. Her regular visits to the state School for the Blind gave her much pleasure. The children welcomed her eagerly, and entertaining for them was a real joy. Now with Teene as her companion, their reception was overwhelming. Elizabeth resolved to do all in her power to assist the youthful blind in obtaining suitable dogs.

Life was full and challenging. Elizabeth was thrilled by the many requests for appearances of the Sextette that came from cities throughout the southwest. And because it meant more freedom for rendering other services without charge, she was pleased when increasing demand for use of the Easter cantata promised some financial return.

In 1936 additional security came when the state legislature voted to purchase the state song which had been adopted years before and to pay the composer a monthly income for her lifetime. Now she was free to devote her time to composing, entertaining and extended public service. From 1931 to 1935 she served on the Board of Regents of the New Mexico School for the Blind.

It was a welcome and unexpected bonus, a confirmation of Elizabeth's belief that a way is provided, when one has faith.

Epilogue

Many exciting changes took place during Elizabeth Garrett's lifetime: the development of vaccines which would have saved her sister Ida's life and prevented Poe's being a cripple; increased knowledge that might have saved her from blindness; law and order, for which her father gave his life, established in the state; radio, broadcasting her voice and carrying music over the world; the flying machine commonly used; Seeing Eye dogs for the blind; the infancy of television; the explosion of the first atomic bomb near the historic great White Sands, marking the beginning of the nuclear age; and to her sorrow, another world war.

When war was declared after the bombing of Pearl Harbor she once again gave benefit programs for the Red Cross, entertaining in hospitals and Army camps. In the final year of the war, she lost a beloved friend, when Teene died after her full lifetime of devoted service to the mistress she adored.

Teene was buried in the grassy patio of *La Casita*. The grave was covered with a concrete slab in which the single word TEENE was inscribed.

Again, Elizabeth made the trip to Morristown. This time she chose to train with a boxer, named Tinka, who was quite different from Teene in disposition, but completely trustworthy in harness. Tinka's irrespressible frolicsomeness was an integral part of her make-up, just as Teene's dignity and wisdom were a part of hers.

It was not long until Roswellites were saying, "Miss Garrett is back with her new dog. She doesn't look at all like Teene." For many, Tinka never supplanted Teene. But the errands, marketing, exercising, and other excursions went on, with Tinka loyally serving the mistress she, too, adored.

On the night of October 16, 1947, the newly organized Kennel Club of Roswell held a meeting in a local church basement. Elizabeth was one of the club's most enthusiastic members.

Although other members came without their canine "best friends," no one questioned the presence of the young female boxer at the side of her mistress.

"My nose tells me we have candles burning tonight," Elizabeth said, soon after her arrival, and she was told that the entire town was without lights because of a power failure.

"I think we should see you home," a friend insisted when the meeting ended.

"Oh, no," Elizabeth protested, "why should you? Tinka will see me safely home, as always."

"But the black-out is still on, there isn't a single street light burning!"

Elizabeth laughed in genuine amusement. "You forget,

darkness means nothing to Tinka and me."

Her friends felt vaguely disturbed, however, and decided a few minutes after her departure to follow and be sure of her safety.

They found her where she had fallen, only a short distance away, her faithful dog cowering and trembling beside her. Friends believed she was the victim of a sudden stroke or heart attack, although the death certificate read "Death caused by a fall."

Friends recalled later that she had once said: "My prayer is, Dear Lord spare me from being a burden to anyone. To be aged and dependent is a sad state, indeed, for any person; but hardest of all for the sightless."

Her prayer had been answered. Independent and productive to the end, she had taken a unique place of her own among the most respected and beloved citizens of the Southwest.

A simple marker at her grave in a Roswell cemetery bears the inscription:

ELIZABETH GARRETT

1947

O FAIR NEW MEXICO

BIBLIOGRAPHY

BOOKS

Garrett, Pat F., *The Authentic Life of Billy the Kid, the Noted Desperado of the Southwest*. Norman: University of Oklahoma Press, 1954, 156 p.

Gibson, Arrel M., *The Life and Death of Colonel Albert Jennings Fountain*. Norman: University of Oklahoma Press, 1965, 310 p.

Keleher, William A., *Violence in Lincoln County, 1869-1881; A New Mexico Item*. Albuquerque: University of New Mexico Press, 1957, 390 p.

Keller, Helen A., *Midstream, My Later Life*. New York: Sun Dial Press, 1937, 362 p.

Scouller, Mildred Marshall, *Women Who Man Our Clubs*. Philadelphia: John C. Winston, 1934, 221 p.

Shinkle, James D., *Reminiscences of Roswell Pioneers*. Roswell, N.M.: Hall-Poorbaugh Press, 1966, 270 p.

Texas State School for the Blind, *Catalogue: List of Graduates*. Austin, 1904.

Wright, Anna Marie Rose and Richard Jones, *Children of the Nineties*. New York: Grossett and Dunlap, 1936, 124 p.

MANUSCRIPTS

Rees, May, *Notes From the Journal of*.

NEWSPAPERS

The Albuquerque (New Mexico) Tribune

The Chicago Inter-Ocean

The El Paso (Texas) Herald-Post

The Las Cruces (New Mexico) Citizen

The New York Sun

The Quincy (Massachusetts) Patriot Leader

The Roswell (New Mexico) Daily Record

RUTH K. HALL

Ruth Kennedy Hall, a native of Oklahoma, came to New Mexico as a young teacher, married, and remained to bring up her family in Las Cruces (where she knew the Garretts) and Albuquerque.

When her children were grown, she turned to a long suppressed desire to try free lance writing. In the 1960s, she was a frequent contributor to *New Mexico Magazine*, and subsequently her articles and fiction have appeared in *Contemporary, Woman's Day, The Sign, Southwest Heritage, Western Review, Ideals,* and other publications.

She is also author of more than fifty published poems, and has been included in several Poetry Anthologies.

Mrs. Hall has won state and national awards in article and fiction writing from the National Federation of Press Women, as well as awards in poetry from the National Federation of State Poetry Societies. She is a member of the National League of American Pen Women, and is listed in *International Who's Who in Poetry*, published in Cambridge, England.